Cistercian Fathers Series: Number Ten

Bernard of Clairvaux

THE LIFE AND DEATH OF SAINT MALACHY THE IRISHMAN

Bernard of Clairvaux

the life
of

CISTERCIAN FATHERS SERIES | NUMBER TEN

L. S. Cunningham
Notre Dame - 1998

[Gift of Br. Patrick Hart, OCSO —
Gethsemani - June 4, 1998]

and death
saint malachy
the irishman

Translated and annotated by ROBERT T. MEYER

CISTERCIAN PUBLICATIONS | Kalamazoo, Michigan | 1978

A translation from the Latin of five works by Bernard of Clairvaux: *Vita Sancti Malachiae episcopi, Epitaphium de Sancto Malachia, Hymnus de Sancto Malachia, Sermo in transitu Sancti Malachiae,* and *Sermo de Sancto Malachia,* made from the critical edition by Jean Leclercq and H. M. Rochais, *Sancti Bernardi Opera,* III, V, VI/1 (Rome: Editiones cistercienses, 1963, 1968, 1970).

Bernard of Clairvaux (1090–1153)
Malachy O'Morgair (1094–1148)

The work of Cistercian Publications
is made possible in part by support from
Western Michigan University
to The Institute of Cistercian Studies

Available from
Cistercian Publications (Distribution)
Saint Joseph's Abbey
Spencer, Massachusetts 01562-1233

Cistercian Publications (Editorial)
Institute of Cistercian Studies
Western Michigan University
Kalamazoo, MI 49008

Library of Congress Cataloging in Publication Data

Bernard of Clairvaux, Saint, 1091?-1153.
    The life of Saint Malachy.

    (Cistercian Fathers series ; no. 10)
    Includes index.
    Translation of Vita Sancti Malachiae
    1. Malachy O'Morgair, Saint, 1094?-1148. 2. Catholic
Church–Bishops–Biography. 3. Bishops–Ireland–
Biography. 4. Christian saints–Ireland–Biography.
I. Title
BX4700.M23B4713   282'.092'4 [B]   78-768
ISBN 0-87907-910-X

TABLE OF CONTENTS

THE LIFE AND DEATH OF SAINT MALACHY THE IRISHMAN

§

INTRODUCTION

THE IMPORTANCE of Saint Malachy for the ecclesiastical history of Ireland can only be understood if we go back several centuries before his day. Ireland was converted to Christianity in the early fifth centuries by missionaries who came from Britain, but had been educated in France and Italy. They brought with them a classical Latin educational background and set up seats of learning and piety in their monastic centers. No doubt they taught the native Irish to write down their traditional lore and very wisely allowed them to keep many of their older customs when such did not interfere with the newer Christian teachings.

For some three centuries Christianity flourished there, but in the meanwhile there were great political and social upheavals in continental Western Europe because of the fall of the Roman Empire, the barbarian invasions, and wars between small kingdoms. During this troublesome period Ireland earned the name of 'Isle of Saints and Scholars'. Christians from the continent came to Ireland for instruction in the humanities and Christian doctrine. The Venerable Bede tells us how English scholars went to Ireland and there received free tuition as well as room and board. Later these scholars were to return to the continent to re-establish Christianity where it had been extirpated. This was also the period of the great Irish missionaries: Saint Columbanus set out from Bangor in North Ireland, went to France to establish monastic foundations there and gradually moved to Italy, where he died in 615, after establishing the Abbey of Bobbio. He had left Saint Gall in the Alps on the way and his hermitage later grew into the great abbey which still bears his name. Later Irish missionaries penetrated farther inland, into Germany and even, in the ninth century, to Kiev in Russia.

After this brilliant period, Ireland herself was to fall prey to the invasion of the Danes in the ninth century. Monasteries were burnt, books and libraries were destroyed, priests and bishops and religious

3

were murdered. There was no strong central government, and the petty chieftains either were murdered or spent their time in fighting amongst themselves and were unable to present a united front against the enemy. The Danes were finally defeated at the Battle of Clontarf in 1014, but this was followed by civil wars amongst the Irish. Church and society at large suffered from these outrages for three centuries. Then at the close of the eleventh century was born in 1094 one Maedoc O'Morgair, who later took the name of Malachy when he entered religion. He received his first education from his father at Armagh, the great center of Irish piety and learning. He was ordained to the priesthood five years before the usual age because his bishop wished to make him his vicar. He then preached the Gospel and worked very hard to bring the people back to a Christian way of life. He re-established marriage as a Christian sacrament and brought back the sacraments of Penance and Confirmation and other modes of ecclesiastical discipline. He instituted once more the regular recitation of the Divine Office in choir—all these pious customs had disappeared. He went for further study to learn the canons of the church councils and correct liturgical practices from Bishop Malchus. He found many irregularities in church administration: his own uncle was lay-abbot at Bangor and appointed For several generations this monastic function had had hereditary leaders: families stayed in power over a long period of time.

Malachy became Bishop of Connor when but thirty years of age and he soon turned a heathen people back to a Christian way of life. About 1128 he was driven from North Ireland to Munster and he established an abbey at Iveragh in West Kerry. Before Saint Celsus of Armagh died, he sent Malachy his crozier as a sign that he should succeed him as bishop there, in order to break a long line of hereditary bishops. Malachy met with such opposition from a warring faction that it was not until 1134 that he could take over his own diocese. Almost at once he consecrated Gelasius as Archbishop of Armagh in order to retire to the smaller poor diocese of Down to lead a monastic life. In 1140 he went to Rome and asked for the *pallium* for the Archbishops of Armagh and Cashel, the two metropolitan sees of Ireland. It was during this trip that he stopped by Clairvaux and met Saint Bernard. So impressed was he with the Cistercian way of life that at Rome he asked to be relieved of his bishopric to become a simple monk and disciple of Saint Bernard. But Pope Innocent II told him that he was needed in Ireland as a leader in the Church. On his return he again made a detour to visit Saint Bernard and he left four of his disciples at

Clairvaux to learn the Cistercian customs. They later came back to Ireland and founded Mellifont Abbey from which other foundations were later made. Whilst in Rome Malachy had been named as papal legate over all Ireland and he carried out this office with great zeal and fervor. He brought all Ireland under the Roman ecclesiastical discipline, bringing to an end the older Celtic liturgies.

In 1148 a synod was held in Ireland and formal application was made for the *pallia* for the two archbishops. Malachy was deputed to go to Pope Eugene, who was in France at the time, but he was delayed by the King of England who forbade his crossing. He arrived in France too late to meet the Pope there and again journeyed to Clairvaux, having previously prophesied that he would die there on All Souls' Day. He arrived there in mid-October and said Mass with great fervor on the Feast of Saint Luke, 18 October, intending to set out that same day for Rome. But he sickened and on 2 November, 1148, died, surrounded by the entire community. Saint Bernard himself celebrated the funeral Mass and a sudden inspiration came to him: at the post-communion he sang the prayer for a confessor-bishop rather than for a dead bishop. This was truly a 'canonization of a saint by a saint' and it was solemnly approved by Pope Clement III in 1190. Saint Malachy is the first formally canonized Irish saint.

Our sources for the Life of Saint Malachy from the Irish Annals are very meagre. Only one date in his life is certain, the day of his death given by Saint Bernard, who was an eye-witness. The *Annals of the Four Masters* mention him as a good and holy man who died in 1148. The *Annals of Inisfallen* and the *Annals of Ulster* both have large *lacunae* for the mid-twelfth century. Saint Bernard's account then must remain the principal document. Besides this we have two sermons given by Saint Bernard: the first at the time of his funeral, and another a year later on the anniversary of his death. There are also extant three letters written by Bernard to Malachy in regard to establishing the Cistercian Order in Ireland. Saint Bernard had conversed with Malachy on the two occasions of his visits to Clairvaux in 1140. He would have heard much about him from the companions whom Malachy had left behind to learn the Cistercian way of life. Bernard was in an ideal situation to give us a first-hand account of Malachy. But in the composition of the *Vita Sancti Malachiae* he was attempting something new to him; we have letters from him—about five hundred altogether— homilies, commentaries, treatises on mystical theology. But although he was here writing what was for him a different type of literary genre, he was only working in a well-established medium, that of hagiography.

Lives of the Saints were frequently read in monastic refectories or privately. We have examples of reading of saints' lives as early as Saint Augustine's *Confessions,* where he tells us that he had been inspired by Saint Athanasius' *Life of Antony of Egypt,* which he probably read in the Latin translation of Evagrius. In later times Saint Gregory the Great had written of the *Life of Saint Benedict* in his *Dialogues.* Then there was Sulpicius Severus' *Life of Saint Martin of Tours,* a text so holy that it was copied into the great Book of Armagh along with the Gospels and the Life of Saint Patrick. Lives of the saints are also to be found in more condensed form in the lessons of the night office of Matins, and at Prime at dawn a brief mention of all the saints of that day was made in the reading of the martyrology. In his daily reading a monk might often have read in a saint's life as part of his *lectio divina,* which included not only scriptural passages and commentaries, but anything we should today include under 'spiritual reading'.

The purpose of the *vita* was to edify. A prologue prefixed to the composition generally tells us that the author had been asked to give an account of some pious person who had died in the state of sanctity. He often protests his inability to write a good account: his Latin is too poor, he is unskilled in literary composition. But he will write under obedience and to praise God's wonderful grace working in a human being. When a miracle is performed we are reminded that it was God's own working through the agent of a person who was very close and dear to him. Crowds of converts are often made by the working of a miracle. Herein a hagiographical document differs from the modern biography, which gives us factual information of a person's birth, life and death. In the *Vita Sancti Malachiae* Saint Bernard is giving us the model of what a bishop should be. His love of poverty, his disdain of ecclesiastical honors, his love of the sick and the poor are all highlighted. Malachy's victories over worldly princes who sought to take away church property or to intimidate him are all mentioned without any reference to exact dates or persons. This information must be sought in contemporary annals or chronicles which are at best often very sketchy.

It may be said that the *Vita Sancti Malachiae* differs from the ordinary saint's lives in that it shows Saint Bernard's profound knowledge of Sacred Scripture, which he quotes from memory as he writes. When he describes the state of barbarity in which Malachy found the Irish we wonder whether he is not indulging in literary hyperbole. At another time he takes a sly dig at his own people for erecting overly ornate cathedrals so out of keeping with Cistercian simplicity. His quotations and reminiscences of such classical authors as Vergil, Horace, Ovid and Apuleius are witness to the literary studies of his youth. One does not fancy Bernard poring over Ovid's *Art of Love* in the cloister at Clairvaux. And when he quotes Boethius' *Consolation of Philosophy* he shows that the 'Last of the Fathers' had read in the 'First of the Scholastics'.

I wish to express my gratitude to the Rt Rev. Edward McCorkell ocso, Abbot of Our Lady of the Holy Cross Abbey, Berryville, Virginia, who has taken an interest in this translation and given me encouragement.

ROBERT T. MEYER
Emeritus Professor of Celtic
Catholic University of America

Harpers Ferry,
West Virginia

Bernard of Clairvaux

THE LIFE OF SAINT MALACHY

TEXT

PREFACE

I T WAS ALWAYS considered praiseworthy to record the illustrious lives of the saints so that they could serve as a mirror and good example; they could be as it were a relish for the life of men on earth.* In this way they are still alive among us, even after death.† They call back to the true life many of those who are dead while they live.† Now indeed the very rarity of holiness requires it, since our age is only too lacking in holy men. We are so aware of this need at present that we are all doubtlessly struck by that saying: Because iniquity shall abound the love of many shall grow cold.* And I suspect that he is already at hand, or at least close by, of whom it was written: Want shall go before his face.† Unless I am mistaken this is Antichrist, whom famine and sterility of all good precedes and accompanies. Then whether he is the messenger of one already here or a presage of one still to come, the need is all too evident. I say nothing of the mob or of the vile crowd of the sons of this world;* I prefer that you look up at the very pillars of the Church.* Whom can you point out to me, even of the crowd of those who seem to be given for a light to the Gentiles,* who is not a smoldering rather than a blazing light? And he says: If the light that is in you is darkness, how great is that darkness.* Unless of course—something I hardly believe—you should say that they are the light who suppose that

*Jb 7:1.

†Si 48:12.

†1 Tm 5:6.

*Mt 24:12.

†Jb 41:13

*Lk 16:8

*Gal 2:9

*Is 49:6

*Mt 6:23

11

†1 Tm 6:5

*Ph 2:21;
  1 Co 13:5

*Mt 5:47

*Lk 3:14

*Is 24:2

*1 Tm 6:8

†Ps 37:31

*Ps 12:1

†Rv 14:3

*Jo 5:35

gain is godliness.† They are the ones who seek in the
Lord's inheritance not the things of the Lord but
their own.* Why should I say: which are their own?
He should be perfect and holy even while holding his
own and seeking his own, provided he keeps his
heart and hands off the possessions of others. Nevertheless he who in his own estimation has proceeded
this far should remember that the same degree of
holiness is also to be expected of a Gentile.* Isn't it
true that soldiers are commanded to be content with
their wages,* that they might be saved? Now it is
a great thing even for a doctor of the Church[1] if he
should be one of the soldiers, or surely, what the
prophet says in reproaching them: if it be with the
priest as with the people.* What a degradation! Is he
really to be esteemed highest who fell from the top-
most position and clings to the lowest lest he be lost
in the abyss? How rare this is even among the clergy.
Show me the man who is content with bare necessities, who despises superfluities! Yet this law was
handed down from the Apostles to their successors:
'having food and raiment,' said they, 'let us be content with these.'* Where is this notion? We find it in
books but not in men. Yet you know of the just man
that the law of his God is in his heart,† not in a
book. That is not the gait of perfection. He who is
perfect is prepared to go without necessities. But
that is beside the point. If only some moderation
could be put on superfluous things. Would that we
did not desire the ends of the earth! Then what?
Could you find anyone who could do this? It would
be hard; see what we have done. We were seeking out
the best man, someone who could save many. We have
a hard time finding one who can save himself. The
best man today is the one who is not entirely evil.

Therefore, since the godly man has vanished*
from the earth, I will not seem redundant in recalling
Bishop Malachy from those who were redeemed from
the earth.† He was a man truly holy, a man of our
own time, of outstanding wisdom and virtue, a
burning and a shining light* still not quenched, but
only withdrawn. Who should have cause to be

angry at me if I bring it back again? Surely there is no one, neither our contemporaries or men of coming generations,* but who would be thankful to me if I recall by my pen someone of whom the world was not worthy,† if I were to preserve for men's memory someone whose memory may be blessed* by all who deign to read it. If I should awaken my sleeping friend, the voice of the turtle shall be heard in our land² saying: 'Lo, I am with you all days, even unto the end of the world.'*

 Then, too, he was buried here.† This is our special duty. The saint held me among his special friends, and in such regard that I could believe I was second to no one in that portion of glory.* Nor is my familiarity with such holiness without its own reward; I already enjoy its first-fruits. In his last moments—rather I should say his first moments according to Holy Scripture: when a man has finished then he is only at the beginning*—I ran up to him so that the blessing of him who was about to die might come upon me.† He, although he could no longer move his limbs, but was strong enough to give his blessing, raising his holy hands above my head blessed me.* That blessing I have inherited†; how now could I be silent about him?

 Finally, you beseech me to undertake this task, Abbot Congar,³ my revered brother and sweet friend, and with you—since you write from Ireland—all that Church of the Saints* which is yours.⁴ Willingly will I accede to your wishes, especially since you desire not an eloquent declamation but a straightforward narrative. I shall give it my attention so that it shall be trustworthy and clear, informing the devout and not burdening the squeamish. Surely the truth of the narrative is certain as far as I am concerned since you yourselves have provided information for me and certainly you would have given me nothing that did not smack of the truth.

*Ps 22:31

†Heb 11:36
*Si 45:1

*Mt 28:20
†Cf. Life ¶75

*2 Co 3:10, 11:17

*Si 18:6

†Jb 29:13.

*Lk 24:30
†1 P 3:9

*Si 31:11

THE LIFE OF SAINT MALACHY

SAINT MALACHY'S PLACE OF BIRTH, HIS PARENTS AND HIS BOYHOOD

OUR MALACHY was born in Ireland of a barbarous tribe; there he was brought up and educated.[5] Yet he betrayed not a mite of his rude origin, any more than a fish of the sea preserves a salty savor. How delightful it is that crude barbarism should have given us so worthy a man, a fellow-citizen with the saints and a true member of the House of God.* He brought honey *Eph 2:19* out of the rock and oil out of the flint.† His parents †Dt 32:13 were noble by their own ancestry and in power, as the word is applied to great men in the world.* His *2 S 7:9* mother was far more noble in her mind than in her lineage. She busied herself at the very beginning of his path,* pointing out to the young child the paths *Pr 8:22* of life.† She regarded this wisdom as much more *Ps 16:11* valuable than mere worldly knowledge.[6] But he had ability for both types of learning, as befitted his age: at school he was taught letters, at home the fear of the Lord.* Day by day he responded to both his *Ps 34:1* teacher[7] and to his mother. He certainly enjoyed a good spirit* from the very first, for he was a *Ws 8:19* teachable and a lovable child, wonderfully obliging in all things. From his mother's breast[4] he was imbibing the waters of saving wisdom† instead of †Si 15:3 milk[8] and day by day he waxed more prudent.

15

*Rm 9:1,
2 Cor 12:6

Should I say more prudent or rather more holy? If I should say both, I'll have no occasion for regret, for I should speak the truth.* He had the manners of an old man. Although still a boy in years, there was not the levity of a boy in him. And although he was regarded with reverence and awe by everyone, still he was not overbearing as so often happens, but he was quiet and subdued in all meekness.* He was not impatient with his tutors nor did he avoid discipline. He was not adverse to reading nor was he a lover of the games in which youth takes such delight. He excelled everyone of his own age† in the rudiments of learning most suitable for one of his years. He soon outdid his teachers* in the matter of discipline and the practice of virtue; in this case his anointing* rather than his mother taught him. Then he took to exercising himself in divine things by seeking solitude, keeping vigils,* meditating on the law,† eating sparingly, praying frequently. Since he could not spend long intervals in church because of his studies, and he really preferred not to because of his modesty, he lifted up holy hands everywhere,* stretching them out to heaven. Of course he did this in secret, for he was careful to avoid the risk of vain-glory which is the poison of virtue.[9]

*1 P 2:18,
Eph 4:2

†Gal 1:14

*Ps 119:99
*1 Jn 2:20

*Ps 77:6
†Ps 1:2

*1 Tm 2:8

¶2. There is a village near the city[10] where the boy was studying and there his teacher used to go with him alone. While they were both going along, as he told us afterwards, he was wont to step back, stop a moment[11] and, standing behind his teacher (who was not aware of it) stretching forth his hands towards heaven,* he used to send up a prayer, quickly as though it were a dart. Then pretending that nothing had happened, he would keep following the teacher. In this way by a kind of pious fraud the boy used to trick the man who was both companion and teacher. I do not intend to mention all the virtues which embellished his early years with the lustre of innate goodness, but rather to hasten on to greater and more edifying matters. But I must relate another incident, because, I think, it showed a sign not only

*1 K 8:22

of good, but also of great, hope in the youth. Once
he was attracted by the reputation of a certain
teacher who was outstanding in what they call the
liberal studies. He went to him intent on such learning; actually he was trying hard to make the best of
his last days at school, and he was panting to begin
advanced studies. But when he reached his house, he
found the man playing with a shoemaker's awl,
cutting up the wall in some strange way with rapid
strokes of the instrument. The lad, being a serious
person, was offended by this, because it betokened a
certain light-mindedness. He left at once, and never
did he show any interest in meeting him again.
Although he was extremely fond of letters he
spurned them, being a lover of virtue. By such a
prelude was he being prepared for what he was to
become in later life, and he was already baiting the
adversary. Thus Malachy spent his youth, passing
through early manhood with a similar simplicity and
purity, except that as he grew, his wisdom and grace
increased with God and man.*   *Lk 2:52*

SAINT MALACHY TOOK GOD AS HIS
TEACHER. HE BECAME A DISCIPLE OF
SAINT IMARUS, CONVERTED MANY, AND
REPROVED HIS OWN SISTER, HE IS
ORDAINED PRIEST AND HE INTRODUCES
INTO THE CHURCH SINGING, WHICH WAS
NOT DONE BEFORE HIS TIME

¶3. From this time on, from his earliest youth, it
began to be more manifest what was in the man* and
it could be seen that the grace of God which was in
him was not vain.* The earnest young man,† perceiving how the world lies in wickedness** and
considering the kind of spirit he had received,* said
to himself:

This is not the spirit of this world. What is it to
this one or that?[12] There is nothing more in common between the one and the other than between
light and darkness.* Mine is from God and I am
aware of what is freely given to me.* Because of this
my gift has been innocence of life up to now, and it
has been my adornment of chastity as well as my
hunger after righteousness.† This has also been my
glory, firm because of its very secrecy, the witness
of my own conscience.* Under the prince of this
world none of these is safe,† since I carry this treasure
in a vessel of clay.* One must be wary lest it be
dashed to the ground and broken and the oil of
gladness* which I carry be poured out. As a matter of
fact it is very difficult not to dash it to pieces, what
with all the rocks and stones of this meandering and
crooked way and life.[13] Shall I lose in a moment all
the blessings of goodness which have anticipated me
from the beginning?* Much rather do I resign myself
and them to him who is their source, for I also belong
to him. I give up my soul* for a time that I may not*

*Jn 2:25

*1 Co 15:10
†1 K 11:28
**Jn 5:19
*Rm 8:15

*1 Co 2:12

*2 Ch 6:14
*2 Ch 2:12

†Mt 5:6

*2 Ch 1:12
†Jn 12:13
*2 Ch 4:7,
  Mk 14:3

*Ps 45:7

*Ps 21:3

*Mt 20:39

lose it eternally. What I am and what I have, where
would they both be safe if not in the hands of the
Author? Who is so solicitous for their preservation, so
powerful to keep them and so faithful in restoring
them? He will preserve them in safety and bring them
back in his own good time. Without restraint I give
myself over to serve him by his own gifts. I surely
cannot lose anything of all that I expend in acts of
piety. It might well be that I could hope for some-
thing beyond. He who is himself a free giver is apt to
repay with interest.* So it is: he will even compound   *Mt 25:27
and multiply virtue in my soul.*   *Ps 138:3
So he thought and acted, knowing full well that
men's thoughts without action are vanity.*   *Ps 94:11

¶II.4. There was a man in the city of Armagh—the
one where Malachy was raised—a man of holy and
austere life, a relentless discipliner of his body.*   *1 Co 9:27
He had a cell close by the church and he lived there,
serving God with fastings and prayers day and
night.† Malachy went to him to take upon himself a   †1 Tm 5:5
rule of life from someone who had condemned him-
self to a living death.[14] Look at his humility: from his
earliest years he had God as his teacher in holy
living, no doubt about that. Then what does he do but
become the pupil of a man, himself a man meek and
lowly in heart.* Even if we had not been aware of it,   *Mt 11:29
he proved it to us himself by this alone. Those who
have tried to teach what they have not learned,
heaping to themselves disciples,* should read this.   *2 Tm 4:3
Those who have never been disciples themselves are
only blind leaders of the blind.* Malachy, taught by   *Mt 15:14
God,† nevertheless sought out a man as a teacher and   †Jn 6:45,
he did so cautiously and wisely. Now I ask: what   Is 54:13
likelier way could he have chosen to give or to show
definite proof of his own progress? Should the exam-
ple of Malachy be only a very small thing* for them,   *1 Co 4:3
they should consider what Paul did. Was it not his
judgment that the Gospel which he had received
from Christ and not from men* be discussed with   *Gal 1:11-12
men, lest perhaps he was running or had run in
vain?* Where he was not sure of himself, neither   *Gal 2:2

am I. If everyone is,[15] he should look to see whether
it is rashness rather than confidence. But these things
need not detain us here.

¶5. Now what happened was noised about the
city,† which was completely taken by surprise at this
novel event. Everyone was astonished and wondered*
at his virtue, much more so because it was not usual
among uncouth people. Then you could see that
thoughts were being revealed out of the hearts of
many.* Many of them considered the act from a
human aspect and grieved and wept to see a youth so
delicate and so beloved of all undertake such strict
practices. Some, suspecting that he did this heed-
lessly, because of his tender age, had no faith in his
perseverance and feared that he would fail in his
resolution. Not a few blamed it on his rashness and
angrily reproached him with having undertaken,
without anyone's counsel, a foolhardy task far
beyond his age and strength. But he did nothing
uncounselled.* He had counsel from the Prophet
who said: It is good for a man that he bear the yoke
in his youth. And he adds: He sits alone and keeps
silence because he has borne it upon him.* The
youth sat at the feet of Imar* (for that was the man's
name) and he either learned obedience† or showed
that he had learned it. He sat quietly, meekly, and
humbly. He sat and kept silence,* knowing that,
according to the Prophet, silence is the ornament of
righteousness.* He sat in perseverance, he kept
silence in modesty, but in that very silence he was
speaking along with holy David into the ears of God:
I am a youth and despised, yet I do not forget your
precepts.* And he sat all alone for awhile, because he
had neither companion nor exemplar. Who before
Malachy had contemplated attempting the very strict
way of life of that man? Everyone admitted how
marvellous it was, but no one dared imitate him.
Malachy showed how it could be done merely by
sitting and keeping silent. Within a few days he had
drawn not a few imitators, encouraged by his example. So he was sitting alone* at first and the only

†Mt 21:20
*Ac 2:12

*Lk 2:35

*Si 32:24

*Lm 3:27-28
*Ac 22:3
†Heb 5:8

*Lm 3:28

*Is 32:17

*Ps 119:141

*Lm 3:28

begotten of his father* soon became one among
many; from being the only-begotten he became the
first-born among many brethren.* And just as he was
before them in his conversion, so also was he more
sublime in his conversation;[16] and he who had come
before them all was in their judgment also above
them all in his virtue. He was deemed worthy by his
bishop[17] and his teacher[18] to be promoted to the
rank of deacon. And they constrained him* [to
accept it].

¶III.6. Hence the Levite of the Lord[19] made public
acclamation and applied himself to every work of
piety, but he showed a predilection for such deeds as
might be considered beneath his notice. For example,
he eagerly helped in burying the poor; not only did it
seem to him a humble, but also a humanitarian
task.[20] Now the ancient temptation from woman was
not missing in the case of our new Tobias,* or
better, the temptation from the Serpent through
woman.* His sister expressed her abhorrence of his
undignified task—for so it seemed to her—and she
said: 'What are you doing, you idiot? Let the dead
bury the dead.'* She kept up her nagging day after
day,† but he answered the foolish woman according
to her own folly:* 'Wretched woman, you keep to
the pure word,* but you are unaware of its meaning.[21]

So he kept devotedly to the office to which he had
been coerced and carried out his work untiringly.
Thus it was they deemed him worthy to be ordained
as a priest.[22] And so it was done.* He was about
twenty-five years old when he was ordained.[23] If it
should seem that the formulary of the canons was
disregarded in either ordination (and certainly he was
ordained to the levitical ministry before his twenty-
fifth year and to the dignity of the priesthood before
his thirtieth year) it can be laid to the zeal of the
ordaining prelate and to the merits of the ordinand
himself.[24] I myself believe it ought not to be condemned when we are dealing with a saint, nor should
a person who is not a saint claim early ordination.

Jn 1:14, 18

Rm 3:29

Lk 24:29

Tb 12:12

Gn 3:1-6

Mt 8:22
†Tb 2:23*
Pr 26:5
Ps 12:6

*Gn 1:7, 9,
15, etc.*

*Lk 8:5
†Ps 43:1
*Si 45:6

†Rm 7:9

*Rm 12:11

*Jr 1:10
†Ps 61:8
*Is 40:4, Lk 3:5
†Ps 19:5
*Ps 104:4
†Ps 74:6

*Ps 78:49

*Dt 7:16,
 Ezk 5:11

*Rv 6:13
†Ps 1:4, 18:42

*Gn 17:14

*probably
 Armagh
†Probably the
 Monastery of
 SS. Peter and
 Paul

The bishop was not satisfied with this, but he entrusted him with his own office of sowing the holy seed* in a nation which was not holy.† He was commissioned to give the law of life and discipline* to an uncultured people who were living without law.† Malachy accepted the command eagerly, fervent in spirit* as he was, nor did he hide away his talents, but he was gasping for gain.[25] Now look! He began to uproot with the hoe of his tongue, to destroy, to scatter* from day to day,† rendering the crooked straight and the rough places plain.* He rejoiced as a giant to run everywhere.† You might say he was a fire burning the briars* of crime. You might say he was an axe or a mattock hacking down† bad sprouts[26] in uprooting barbarous rites, supplanting them with the Church's. He abolished all outmoded superstitions (the place abounded with them) and wherever he found them, he drove out tribulations sent by evil angels.*

¶7. Finally, his eye did not spare* whatever he found disorderly, unsightly, or deformed, but as the hail scatters the unripe fruit from the fig tree* and the wind scatters the dust from the face of the earth† so he strove with all his power to expel such things from his presence and from his people.* Beneficent legislator that he was, he substituted heavenly laws in their place. He laid down laws filled with justice, moderation and honesty. He established again the apostolic sanctions and rulings of the holy fathers and in particular the customs of the Holy Roman Church.[27] From that time to this they observe chanting and psalm-singing at the canonical hours according to universal custom. There was very little of this done before that, even in the city.* While a boy he had learned singing and he soon introduced song into his monastery† at a time when no one in the city or in the bishop's retinue knew how to sing or even cared. Then, too, Malachy re-instituted[28] that most wholesome use of confession, the sacrament of confirmation and the marriage contract—something again about which they knew nothing and cared less. But these examples must suffice, for throughout this whole narrative we must pass over many things in order to be brief.

HOW HE SOUGHT OUT BISHOP MALCHUS
AND BEFRIENDED A KING IN FLIGHT
AND RESTORED HIM TO HIS KINGDOM

¶IV.8. Since Malachy was eager and full of zeal lest, regarding ritual and the proper veneration of the sacraments, he should lay down a law or teach anything that went counter to the universal Church, he made up his mind to visit Bishop Malchus[29] who might give him fuller information about all these things. He was an old man full of days* and virtues, and the wisdom of God was in him.† He was Irish by birth but it was in England he converted to the monastic habit and intention, at Winchester monastery. From there he was raised to episcopal rank at Lismore, a Munster town.* Among the various cities of that realm this was one of the more noble. So much grace from above had been given him that he was famous not only for his way of life and his teaching but also for signs. Here I shall quote but two examples so that it will be apparent to everyone what sort of teacher Malachy had in the knowledge of holy things.*

He healed a lad afflicted with a mental condition— they call them lunatics—while confirming him with holy unction. The boy's cure was well known and certain; he was soon made porter to his house and stayed on in that capacity until he reached manhood. To another who was deaf he gave hearing, at which the deaf person declared marvellously that when the saint put his finger into each of his ears* he felt two little things like piglets come out of them. Because of these and other like deeds his fame spread and he gained so great a name* that Scots[30] and Irish met with him and he was treated as father by both. Malachy set out to visit this man with the blessing of

*Gn 35:29, 1 Ch 23:1, Jb 42:16
†1 K 3:28

*today County Waterford.

*Ws 10:10

*Mk 7:33

*2 Sm 7:9

his father Imar and the permission of the bishop.
After a prosperous journey he was kindly received by
the old man. He stayed with him for some years, so
that in that lapse of time he might drink deeply from
his aged breast, being mindful of the proverb: with
the ancient is wisdom.* I have a feeling that the *Jb 12:12*
reason why the Overseer of all things wished to have
his servant Malachy known in so celebrated a place
was that he might be useful to all.[31] For he could
not but be beloved by all who knew him. In the
meanwhile one circumstance at that time showed
men from another quarter that God was recognized* *Rm 1:19*
in him.

¶9. A feud arose between the King of South
Munster,[32] which is a part of Ireland, and his brother.
When the elder brother was victorious,[33] the king
was driven from his domain and fled to Bishop
Malchus. However he did not do this that he might
recover his realm through his aid, but rather the
devout prince gave way to wrath.* He made neces- *Rm 12:19*
sity into a virtue,[34] preferring to lead his life in
private. While the bishop was getting ready to receive
the king with the honor due him, he turned it down,
remarking that he was willing to be considered as one
of those poor brethren who were his companions. He
preferred to lay aside his royal pomp and be content
with common poverty, to look forward to God's will
rather than to recoup his kingdom by force. Nor did
he wish to shed blood* which would cry out to God *Gn 9:6*
from the earth† against him. The bishop rejoiced at †Gn 4:10
hearing this. Astonished at his devotion, he granted
him his wish. What more should I say? To the king is
given a poor little hut to live in and Malachy for a
teacher, bread with salt and water for his food. The
very presence of Malachy served as the king's sweet-
meats. His life and his learning were such that he
could say to him: How sweet are your words, to
my taste, yea, sweeter than honey to my mouth.† †Ps 119:103
addition, every night he watered his bed with his
tears* and he also extinguished the evil burning lust *Ps 6:6
of his flesh with a daily bath of cold water.[35] And

*David the royal
psalmist.
† Ps 25:18

*Ps 66:20
†Si 51:15,
 Ac 10:31

*Ps 37:37

*Ps 103:6;
 146:7

*1 Ch 5:26;
 2 Ch 36:22

*Lk 23:47
†Ac 5:17

*Lk 21:15

*1 M 3:60

*Mk 6:20

the king praying, with the King*, said: Look upon my affliction and my pain, and forgive all my sins.† God did not turn away his prayer nor his mercy from him.* His supplication was heard,† even though in quite a different manner than he had himself intended. Now he was worried about his soul, but God who vindicates the innocent, wishing to show men that there is a remainder for the man of peace,* was meanwhile preparing to execute judgment for the oppressed*—something he had never in his innermost thoughts hoped for. God stirred up the spirit of a neighboring king;* for Ireland is not a single kingdom, but is divided into many.[36] When this king saw what had happened,* he was filled with indignation.† At first he felt anger at the freedom of the robbers and the insolence of the proud, then pity for the desolate kingdom and the rejected king. He went down to the poor man's hut, urging him to come back, but he could not convince him. He kept trying: he promised help, he admonished him not to despair of the result, he prophesied that God would be present, whom all his adversaries would not be able to resist.* He even made special mention of the oppression of the poor and the devastation of the countryside. Even so he did not persuade him.

¶10. Finally he did acquiesce on the command of the bishop and by Malachy's persuasion, for it was in these two men he placed all trust, but he acquiesced only with difficulty. A king follows a king according to the king's own word.[37] As was the will in heaven,* the reavers were easily driven out and the man is brought back with great exultation by all and is restored to his kingdom. From that time the king loved and revered Malachy, especially since he had learned from the holy man what is worthy of veneration and love. He certainly could not be unaware of the holiness of the man whom he was fortunate to have had as a companion in his adversity. And once he was restored to prosperity he continually kept up his acts of friendship and promises and he heard him gladly, and when he heard him did many things.*

Enough about this. However, I think that it was not
accidental that the Lord thus magnified him* in the   *Si 45:2-3
sight of kings,† but it was because he was his chosen   †Ps 119:46
vessel, ready to carry his name before kings
and princes.*   *Ac 9:15

HOW MALACHY SAVED HIS DEAD SISTER
BY THE SACRED OBLATION

¶V.11. In the meanwhile [Malachy's] sister died; we spoke of her earlier. The visions concerning her which he saw should not be passed over. He was so repelled by her carnal life that he vowed he'd never see her in the flesh.* But inasmuch as her flesh was being dissolved, the vow was also dissolved, and he began to see in spirit her whom he would not see in the flesh. One night while dreaming he heard a voice telling him that his sister stood just outside in the yard and had not tasted a thing for thirty whole days. Waking up, he realized in a flash the food for which she was starving. Carefully reckoning the number of days he had heard mentioned, he found it was that very length of time since he had stopped offering the living bread from heaven* on her behalf. Now since it was not his sister's soul but her sin that he hated, he took up once more the good practice which he had laid aside. Nor was it done in vain: not long afterwards he saw her come to the threshold of the church, not yet able to come in and wearing a dark garment. And when he persevered, making sure that no day should deprive her of her accustomed gift, he saw her a second time in an off-white garment, admitted inside the church, but still not allowed close to the altar. Finally the third time she was seen in the midst of the white-clothed choir, arrayed in bright clothing.* Do you understand, reader, how much the fervent prayer of a righteous man avails?† True it is that the kingdom of heaven suffers violence and the violent take it by force.* Would it not seem to you that the prayer of Malachy took the place of a burglar[38] at the very gates of heaven, in that a woman deep in sin* procured through her

*Lk 2:26

*Jn 6:32

*2 M 11:8,
  Ac 10:30,
  Jm 2:2

†Jm 5:16

*Mt 11:12

*Lk 7:37

brother's prowess what was denied her on her
own merits?

Oh good Jesus, you give this power, you who have
suffered; strong and merciful to save, you show
mercy and strength in your arm,* you preserve it in   *Lk 1:51*
your sacrament for the saints who are in the earth,*   *Ps 16:3*
even to the ends of the world.† Certainly the sacra-   †*Mt 28:20*
ment is able to bring sins to nought, to overcome
powers face to face, to bring back to heaven those
returning from earth.

HOW MALACHY RESTORED
THE MONASTERY OF BANGOR
AND CERTAIN MIRACLES

¶VI.12. Now the Lord was surely preparing his beloved Malachy in that region for the glory of His name. For those who had sent him* could no longer put up with his prolonged absence, but sent letters to recall him. Once he had returned, certainly the wiser in everything befitting him, lo! a work prepared and preserved by God for Malachy.* The rich and powerful man who owned Bangor[39] and its holdings, inspired by God, at once gave over into his hands all his property and himself as well.[40] This man was his uncle,[41] but to Malachy kinship of spirit carried more weight than relationship by blood. This prince handed over to Malachy the place Bangor, from which he also took his name,[42] so that he might build, or rather rebuild, a monastery there. There had been there earlier under the first abbot Comgall[43] a very celebrated monastery which produced many thousands of monks, the head of many monasteries. This was a holy place highly productive of saints, bringing forth holy fruit for God very abundantly.* So it came about that one of the sons of that holy congregation, Lugaid[44] by name, is rumored to have founded a hundred monasteries single-handed. I mention this so that the reader may realize from this one instance what a great number of others there were. His plantations[45] so filled both Ireland and Scotland that it seems to have been predicted long before in these verses of David: You visit the earth and bless it; you make it to be productive. The river of God is full of water. You prepare their grain, for you so prepare the earth,

Cellach and Imar; see ¶8.

Eph 2:10

Rm 7:4

blessing the rivers, multiply its shoots, With drops of
rain will it rejoice while causing growth* and so on in   *Ps 65:9-10*
the following verses. Not only did they flow over the
places just mentioned, but this army of saints over-
flowed into foreign territory in the manner of a great
flood.* Saint Columbanus[46] was one of them. Com-   *Lk 6:48*
ing to our Gallish parts, he built a monastery at
Luxeuil and a great people was made there.[47] They
say it was so great a population of monks that choirs
succeeded each other in turn, the solemn offices
went on continually in such a way that there was not
a moment by day or night when praises were not
being sung.

¶13. These were the things related about the
ancient glory of the monastery of Bangor, which was
destroyed by pirates long ago.[48] Yet Malachy embraced the life there because of the reputation of
its former dignity and also because many bodies of
the saints slept there.* He felt that he was somehow   *Mt 27:52*
replanting Paradise.† Not to mention those who were   †Gn 2:8
buried there in peaceful times,* they say that nine   *Si 44:14*
hundred were killed in one day by the pirates.[49] The
holdings of Bangor were extensive,[50] but Malachy
was content with the holy place alone and he
yielded all its possessions and lands to another.
Certainly from the time of the destruction of the
monastery there was always someone who held it
with its possessions. Men were duly elected and even
bore the title of abbot, preserving in name, but not in
fact, that which had once been.[51] When many urged
him not to alienate the possessions, but to keep
everything for himself, this lover of poverty did not
give in, but enjoined election upon another to hold
them as was customary. But the place was held in
trust for Malachy and his monks as we said above.
As it later turned out, he might better have kept it
all,* but he was regarding humility rather than peace.   *See ¶¶61-62.*

¶14. Then at Father Imar's command he took with
him about ten of the brethren and, arriving at the
place, began to build.* It happened one day while he   *Lk 14:30*

was cutting with an axe that one of the workmen accidentally got in his way while he was raising the axe and it fell on his spine with full force. He fell to the ground and everyone rushed up, thinking he was mortally wounded or dead. His tunic was rent from top to bottom.* But the man was found unharmed, his skin so slightly wounded that only a slight scratch appeared on its surface. The man whom the axe had laid out stood up unscathed in the sight and to the amazement of those standing around. Because of this they became more eager and from then on were found more ready for work. This was the beginning of the miracles* which Malachy worked. Within a few days the chapel was finished with polished boards,* firmly and tightly fastened together —an Irish work finely wrought.⁵² And from that time was service rendered in it to God as in the old days—the devotion was the same, the numbers were fewer. Malachy was in charge for awhile, by the appointment of Father Imar⁵³ being both rector and rule for the brethren.* They used to read in his life how they should be converted and he walked before them in justice and holiness in God's presence.†

He did in a singular way many things which were above and beyond the common rules and in this he more than led the way for everyone. No one else could approach him in these more difficult practices. At that time and place there was someone ailing and the devil stood near him and, speaking openly, suggested that he should pay no heed to Malachy's warnings but should attack him with his dagger and kill him if he came in to see him. Once this became known, those who were caring for him told this to Malachy at his instigation and they warned him. But Malachy, taking up only his usual weapon of prayer, made a bold attack on the fiend and put to flight both the disease and the demon. Now the man's name was Malchus.* According to the flesh he is the brother of our Christian, the abbot of Mellifont.⁵⁴ Both of them are still alive, now closer brothers in the Spirit.⁵⁵ Once freed, he was not ungrateful; on the spot he turned to the Lord,* as it were,

*Mt 27:51

*Jn 2:11

*Gn 6:14

*ipse rector,
 ipse regula
 fratrum.
†Lk 1:75-76

*Cf. Jn 18:10

*2 Co 3:16

changing both his habit and his mind.* The brethren
were well aware that the Evil One was jealous of their
well-being. They were edified, but rendered more
cautious about the future.

¶VII.15. Here he also healed a cleric named Michael
who suffered dysentery, sending him something from
his own table as a last resort. Later he cured the same
man when he was grievously stricken with illness a
second time in both body and mind. Immediately he
clung to God* and to his servant Malachy, afraid that
something worse should happen to him* if he were
once again ungrateful for the kindliness and the
miracle. And now—as we have heard—he is the
superior of a monastery in the Scottish parts, and
this was the newest of all the foundations that
Malachy established.[56] From day to day Malachy's
fame and that of his community increased, with his
name great† both inside and outside* [the monas-
tery], but not greater than the fact. He stayed on
there† even after he became a bishop, since the
place was close to the city.[57]

¶VIII.16. The episcopal see was vacant[58] then and
had been so for a long time as Malachy was unwilling
to give his assent even though they had elected him.
They insisted however and after awhile he consented,
when his own teacher[59] joined their entreaties, as did
the metropolitan.* Malachy was barely thirty years
old when he was consecrated bishop and installed at
Connor; that was the name of the city.[60] Once he had
begun to exercise his office the man of God realized
that he had been sent not to men but to beasts.
Never had he known such men, so steeped in barbarism; never had he found people so wanton in their
way of life, so cruel in superstition, so heedless of
faith, lawless, dead-set against discipline, so foul in
their life-style; Christians in name, yet pagans at
heart. They gave no tithes, no first-fruits; they did
not contract legitimate marriage nor make confession; there was neither penitent nor confessor to be
found. There were few to minister at the altar. But

*Cf. RB 58.

*Ps 73:28
*Jn 5:14

†2 S 7:9
*Rv 5:1

†Jn 3:22

*See ¶19

what need was there of more where the small showing
among the laity was practically idle? There was no
hope of a harvest they might reap among so good-for-
nothing a people. In the churches there was heard
neither the preacher's voice nor the singer's chant.
What could the athlete of the Lord do?[61] Either
withdraw in disgrace or fight in danger. But he who
realized that he must be a shepherd and not a mere
hireling* chose to stand his ground rather than
to flee, being prepared to give up his life for his
sheep* if need be. But although they were all
wolves and no sheep, the shepherd stood in their
midst undaunted, ingenious in every ruse by which
to make wolves into sheep.[62] This he accomplished
by admonishing them in a body, arguing privately,
weeping with each individual; sometimes roughly,
sometimes gently, whichever way he saw would be
best for each one. In the cases where he had made
little progress he offered for them a contrite and a
humbled heart.* How many nights he gave over
entirely to vigils, stretching out his hands in prayer![63]
And when they would not come willingly to church
he went about the city* in the highways and the
bywayst seeking earnestly* anyone he might gain
for Christ.

¶17. But he also went out to the country and to
small towns with that holy band of his own disciples
who were never absent from his side. He used to go
and to bestow[64] even on the ungrateful their portion
of the Bread of heaven.* He was not carried on
horseback, but he walked on foot, proving himself
an apostolic man. Good Jesus! What your soldier
suffered in your name* at the hands of wicked
men.† How much he suffered from those very
people to whom and for whom he spoke of your
good things. Who could adequately express how
vexed he was,* how insulted he was,† what injuries
he suffered, how often he was worn out for lack of
food, how often he was afflicted with cold and
nakedness?* Nevertheless, with those who hated
peace he was a peacemaker at all times,* both in

Margin notes:
*Jn 10:11-12
*Jn 10:11
*Ps 51:17
*Ps 59:6, 15
†Lk 14:21
*Sg 3:2
*Lk 12:42
*Ac 9:16
†Is 1:4
*Jr 12:6
†1 Th 2:2
*1 Co 11:27
*Ps 120:7

and out of season.* When cursed he prayed,† when
wrongfully accused he defended himself with the
shield of patience and overcame evil with good.*
But why should he have not conquered? He persevered in knocking* and according to the promise,
to him who knocked it was finally opened.* How
could it be possible that what the Truth† had announced beforehand should not follow? The right
hand of the Lord has done mighty deeds,* because
the mouth of the Lord has spoken the truth.† Their
hardness of heart yielded, their barbarity was quelled;
the disobedient house* began to be relaxed little by
little and gradually it began to allow chastisement
and to receive discipline. Barbarous laws were extirpated and those of Rome introduced. Ecclesiastical
usages are adopted everywhere, pagan customs are
abandoned; churches are rebuilt and clergy are ordained to them. The sacraments are solemnly performed according to their rite, confessions are made,
folk come together in church and the celebration of
marriage dignifies concubinage. In a word so much
have all things changed for the better that today one
could apply to that people what God says through his
prophet: Those who were not my people hitherto,
are now my people.*

¶IX.18. After some years it happened that the
city[65] was destroyed by the king of the northern part
of Ireland, since out of the North comes all evil.*
And perhaps that evil was a good thing for those
who put it to good use. For who knows but that God
wished to wipe out the ancient evils of his own
people by such a scourge? In this way Malachy himself, compelled by necessity,* left with a group of his
disciples. Nor was his exile idle. At this opportunity
the monastery of Iveragh was built and Malachy
entered with up to one hundred and twenty of his
brethren. There King Cormac met him.* He was the
one who had once been driven from his kingdom and
had by the mercy of God received consolation in
Malachy's care.* And that site was located in his
kingdom. The king was delighted to see Malachy and,

*2 Tm 4:2
†1 Co 4:13

*Rm 12:21

*Lk 11:8
*Lk 11:9-10
†Jn 14:6

*Ps 118:15
†Is 1:20, 40:5,
  etc.

*Ezk 2:5-6

*1 P 2:10.
Cf. Ho 2:24.

*Jr 1:14

*1 S 13:12

*Cormac
Mac Carthaig,
king of West
Munster.

*See ¶¶9,10.

grateful in remembering the kindness done to him, he put everything he had at the disposal of Malachy and his monks. Many animals were brought for the use of the brethren, as well as much gold and silver offered with royal generosity towards the expenses of building. He was himself entering and leaving with them,* anxious and ever keen to help—in dress a king but in spirit Malachy's disciple. The Lord blessed that place because of Malachy.* In a short while it became great in worldly goods, possessions and persons. There [Malachy] the bishop and teacher, making as it were a fresh beginning, himself kept strictly the law and discipline which he imposed on others.* In his turn* he used to tend to the task of cook and he served the brethren as they sat at the table.† When the brethren took turns singing or reading in church he did not allow himself to be passed over, but vigorously took his turn as one of them. Not only did he share their holy poverty, he was much more zealous than the others.*

*Ac 9:28

*Gn 39:5

*Si 17:9
*Lk 1:8
†Lk 12:37,
  22:27

*Ga 1:14

HOW HE WAS APPOINTED BEFOREHAND
TO BE THE NEXT ARCHBISHOP AND HOW
HE HANDED OVER TO ANOTHER THE
METROPOLITAN SEE AFTER IT HAD BEEN
FREED FROM MISFORTUNES AND HOW
HE PARTITIONED HIS OWN SEE IN TWO

¶X.19. While all this was happening Archbishop
Celsus, who had ordained Malachy deacon, priest,
and bishop, fell ill. Realizing that death was near* he   ● *1 M 1:6
made a sort of last testament with the provision that
Malachy should succeed him, since no one else
appeared more worthy of the first see.[66] This he
pointed out to those who were present and he commanded it to those who were absent and on the
authority of Saint Patrick he enjoined it especially
on both the kings of Munster,[67] and the elders of the
land. Now [Patrick], who had converted them to the
faith, had been held in great reverence and esteem as
the Apostle of that people. The see over which he
presided while alive and where, now dead, he rests
was held from the very beginning in such veneration
by all the people that not only bishops and priests
and other clerics, but the whole body of kings and
princes is subject to the metropolitan in all obedience and that one man is himself in charge of all.
But the thoroughly evil custom had arisen through
the diabolical ambitions of certain powerful men that
the holy see [of Armagh] was held by hereditary
succession. They allowed none to be consecrated
bishop except those who were of their own tribe and
family. Nor did this abominable succession merely
endure for a short time, but this wickedness persisted
for fifteen generations![68] An evil and adulterous
generation* had entrenched itself by this depraved   *Mt 12:39, 16:4
custom—yea, this wrong which should be punished

by death of any kind—until even though some clerics could not claim blood kinships, with bishops it was quite different.[69]

Before Celsus there had been eight married men who were never ordained, but they were at least literate. This is why there existed those circumstances of which we spoke above and they held for all of Ireland: a total breakdown of ecclesiastical discipline, a relaxation of censure, a weakening of the whole religious structure. Hence cruel barbarity was substituted for christian meekness; as a matter of fact paganism was brought in under the label of Christianity. For a thing unheard of from the very beginning of Christianity occured: bishops were changed without order or reason and they were multiplied at the whim of the metropolitan until one episcopal see was not satisfied with one bishop, but almost every single church had its own bishop.[70] No wonder. For how could the members of so sick a head be healthy?

¶20. Cellach,[71] grieving for this and his people's crimes of this sort—for he was a good and Godfearing man*—took every pain to have Malachy as his own successor, because he was confident that in so doing he would eradicate this badly rooted succession. He was beloved by everyone and someone whom all imitated, and the Lord was with him.* Nor was he frustrated in his hope, for when he died Malachy was put in his place, but not at once, and not easily. Now there was of that worthless seed* a certain Maurice[72] who wished to occupy the post. For a period of five years, relying on secular power,[73] he fastened himself like a leech on the Church, more a tyrant than a bishop. Devout souls were really in favor of Malachy. At last they urged him to submit to the burden according to the arrangements of Cellach. But he who generally refused every honor as something leading to his downfall, seemed to have stumbled onto a good excuse, because at the time it would have been impossible for him to enter the office peaceably. Everyone pressed him toward a work so holy and they begged him, especially the two bishops,

*Lk 2:25

*1 S 18:14

*Is 1:4

Malchus[74] and Gilbert.[75] The former was the superior
of Lismore mentioned earlier, and the latter was the
first to function as legate of the Apostolic See
throughout all of Ireland. These two could no longer
tolerate the adultery of the Church and the dishonor
paid to Christ in the course of three years of
Maurice's presumption and Malachy's indecisiveness.
They convened the bishops and princes of the land
and approached Malachy in one spirit, prepared to
use force. At first he refused, alleging the difficulty of
the situation, the numbers, the sheer strength and the
ambition of that noble family. Should a wee poor
man like himself oppose so many men of such great
quality who had so entrenched themselves and held
out for almost two hundred years, as though they
possessed the sanctuary of God as an inheritance,*   *Ps 83:12*
and now occupied the see? [He said] he would not
be able to root them out, even at the loss of human
lives; it was not his will that men's blood be shed
because of him;* finally [he added] he was already   *Gn 9:6*
joined to another spouse[76] whom he could not
lawfully put away.*   *Mk 10:2*

¶21. But insisting that it was not true and crying
out that the word had come out from the Lord,*   *Gn 24:50*
they commanded him authoritatively to undertake
the duty and they threatened him with anathema.
'You are leading me to death,' said he, 'but I shall
obey with the hope of martyrdom, on this condition: that if, as you believe, this business should turn
out for the better, and God vindicate his inheritance
from those who would destroy it,* then, when the   *Ps 35:10,*
whole affair is settled and the Church is enjoying   *Jr 50:11*
peace, you will permit me to return to my former
spouse, my lady poverty[77] from whom I am being
snatched away, and that I may find for myself here
a substitute who may then be found suitable for
the post.'

Note, reader, the strength of the man and his

Ac 5:41

purity of heart. He did not strive for honor and was not afraid to die for Christ's name.* What could be purer or braver than this intention, that exposing himself to danger and hard work, he should yield the fruit to another—the peace and very security in the place of high office? This he does when by this understanding he keeps for himself a free return to a life of poverty once peace and liberty have been restored to the Church. Once they agreed to this, he gave in to their will, or rather to the will of God by whom what he now grieved to have happen to him had already been foreshown. While Cellach lay ill, there had appeared to Malachy a woman of great stature and reverend appearance[78] and of course, being far away, he knew nothing of Celsus' condition. When he asked her who in the world she was, she replied that she was Cellach's wife. Then she handed him the pastoral staff which she held in her hand and disappeared. Several days later the dying Cellach sent his staff to Malachy, to the man who was to succeed him, and it was then that he realized the meaning of what he had seen. It was the recollection of this vision that particularly terrified Malachy, that by persisting in refusing what he had long avoided, he might seem to be resisting God's holy will.* Still he did not enter the city while the imposter lived, lest he provide an occasion for the murder of those to whom he had come to bring life. And so for two years—as long as the imposter lived on—he remained outside the city exercising his episcopal function throughout the whole province.[79]

Gn 50:19,
Est 13:9

¶IX.22. As soon as that fellow had been carried off by sudden death, a certain Nigellus,* to tell the truth he was very black,[80] quickly grabbed the see again. While still alive, Maurice had made provision for his soul,* by giving him an inheritance by which he, who was going out of his way to be damned, might keep adding to the works of damnation.[81] He was also of the damned race and a kinsman of Maurice.[82] Nevertheless the king and bishops and the faithful of the land came together to bring Malachy

Niall

Jos 9:24

in. And behold over against them the council of the
malignant.* One of the sons of Belial,† ready for evil,
powerful in iniquity,** knowing the place where
they had planned to come together,†† assembled
many and stealthily took over a high hill opposite
the place where they would be dealing with other
things, planning to rush in upon them unawares and
kill the innocent.* They had determined to butcher
the king with the bishop so there would be no one to
avenge innocent bloodshed.* Malachy got wind of
this and entering a church nearby and lifting up his
hands, he prayed to the Lord. There came clouds and
darkness,* and also dark waters and thick clouds,†
turning the day into night.** Lightnings and thun-
derings†† had the awesome spirit of tempests*
threatened the day of Judgment, all nature contrived
to prophesy imminent death.[83]

Ps 22:16
†*Jg 19:22,*
1 S 2:12
***Ps 52:3*
††*Jn 18:2*

Ps 10:8

Rv 19:2

Dt 4:11, Ps 97:2
†*Ps 18:12*
***Jb 17:12*
††*Ex 19:16*
Ps 148:8

¶23. So you may know, reader, that the prayer of
Malachy raised the elements, the tempest fell on only
those who were seeking his life;* the dark whirl-
wind† snatched up only those who had made ready
the works of darkness.* Then the one who had been
the ringleader of the plot died, struck by a thunder-
bolt* with three others—partners in death as they had
been companions in crime. Their bodies were found
the following day half burnt and stinking, each one
stuck fast in the branches of trees where the wind,
having lifted him up, had flung him down.* Three
others were found half alive and the rest had been
scattered in all directions. But those who were with
Malachy, no matter how close they were to the place,
the storm never touched at all nor did any damage.*
In this circumstance we find new proof of the truth
of that saying, that the prayer of the just man
pierces the heavens.* But it is also a new example of
that ancient miracle when long ago all Egypt lay in
total darkness, only Israel remained in the light. As
Scripture has it: Wherever Israel was, there was
light.* Here I recall, too, what the holy Elijah did
once, summoning clouds and showers from the very
ends of the earth,* and again calling down fire from

Ps 38:12, 70:2
†*Jb 3:5-6*
Rm 13:12

2 S 11:15

Ps 102:10

Dn 3:50

Si 35:21

Ex 10:21

1 K 18:45

*2 K 1:10
†Jn 13:31

the heavens on those who mocked him.* So also in
like manner is God glorified in† his servant Malachy.

¶XII.24. It was in the thirty-eighth year of his life
that the poverty-loving Malachy entered Armagh as
the metropolitan bishop of all Ireland,[84] but only
after the usurper had been driven out. Once the king
and others who had brought him in had returned
home, Malachy remained in God's hands,[85] but still
there remained for him combats without and fears

*2 Co 7:5
†1 K 21:4

within.* For lo, the offspring of vipers, raging and
lamenting† that it had been cheated of its inheritance, reared up in a body both inside and outside

*Ps 2:2, Ac 4:26

against the Lord and against his anointed one.*
Furthermore, Niall, seeing that flight was his only
recourse, took with him certain insignia of that see,
namely the text of the Gospels[86] which had been
Saint Patrick's and the staff embellished with gold
and precious stones which people called the 'staff of
Jesus'. (They say that the Lord himself had touched
it with his own hands and had shaped it.)[87] These
were held in the highest esteem and reverence among
these people. Indeed they are very well known and
cherished by the populace and held in such veneration by them all that anyone seen having them is con-

*Dt 32:6
†RB 1

sidered by this foolish and unwise people* to be their
bishop. That man, that gyrovague† and another

*Jb 1:7; 2:2

Satan, went round about the earth and rambled
through it,* carrying the sacred insignia which he
showed off everywhere, and he was everywhere
received because of them, winning everyone's alle-
giance to himself and turning everyone he could
away from Malachy. These are the things he did:

¶25. Now there was a certain prince[88] of the more
powerful of the iniquitous race whom the king had
forced to swear to keep peace with the bishop. This
he did before he left the city and he took many
hostages from him besides. After the king left, however, he entered the city and took counsel with his
relatives and friends how they might take the saint
by treachery and put him to death; but they feared

the people.* Swearing on oath to the murder of   *Mt 26:4, Mk
Malachy, they set the place and the day and a traitor   *14:1, Lk 22:2*
gave them a sign.† On the appointed day when the   †Mk 14:44
bishop was celebrating solemn Vespers in the church
with all the clergy and a great crowd of people, that
vile person sent for him by peaceful words cunningly
wrought,* asking that he should deign to come down   *1 M 1:31,
to him so he might make peace. Those who were   *7:10, 27*
seated nearby said that he ought instead to come to
the bishop, that the church was the more fitting
place to agree on peace terms. They had a presentiment of some trickery afoot. The messengers added
that this was not safe for the prince: he feared for his
own head, and he did not trust the crowds, who some
days previously had almost killed him because of the
bishop. While they were arguing back and forth in
this way, some saying he should go, others that he
should not, the bishop, wanting peace and not fearing
death spoke up: 'Let me go, brethren. Let me
imitate my Master!* I am a Christian to no purpose if   *1 Co 11:1
I do not follow Christ. It may be that by humility I
shall turn the tyrant, but if not I shall still conquer
by showing myself a shepherd to the sheep, the
priest to the layman, something he should have done
for me. And, as much as in me lies, I shall edify you
just a bit by such an example. Suppose it should
happen that I am killed? I should not refuse death*   *Ac 25:11
so that you might have an example of life. As the
Prince of bishops says, it does not behoove a bishop
to lord it over the clergy, but to be an example to his
flock.* We have received no other example from Him   *1 P 5:3
who humbled Himself becoming obedient even to
death.* Who would grant me to leave behind this   *Phil 2:7-8
example sealed with my own blood?[89] Put me to the
test now, to see whether your bishop has learned well
from Christ not to fear death for Christ.'

And getting up, he began to leave while they were
all weeping and beseeching him not to wish so much
to die for Christ that he should abandon so large a
flock of Christ.*   *Phil 1:23

¶26. Placing his whole hope in the Lord,* he went   *Ps 78:6

*Ac 21:13,
Jn 11:16
†Eph 6:16

*Gn 4:6
†Ex 15:16

*Ps 27:2

*Jn 4:37

out speedily, with only three of his disciples, prepared
to die with him.* As he crossed the threshold,[90] himself fortified by the buckler of faith,† he suddenly
found himself in the midst of armed men. The
men's faces fell* as fear so great came over them†
that the Bishop could say: 'My enemies that trouble
me have themselves been weakened and have fallen.'*
This story is true:* you could see the victim standing
there and the executioners fully armed surrounding
him, and there was no one who would sacrifice him.
You would think their arms were bewitched; no one
so much as raised his hand. The one who appeared to
be the ringleader rose up to honor rather than to
assault him.* Fellow, where is the sign you were going to give for the murder of the bishop? This sign
portends reverence rather than death; it delays
death, it does not deliver it. What a marvellous thing!
They offer peace who intended slaughter! He could
hardly refuse peace when he had sought it at the risk
of his life. So peace was made—and so firm a peace
that from that day forward the priest found the
enemy not only subdued, but obedient and even
devoted. When they heard this the faithful rejoiced,
not only because innocent blood was saved that

*Dn 13:62

day,* but because the souls of many evil-intentioned
persons made their escape to salvation on Malachy's
merits. And fear seized all who happened to be

*Lk 5:26, 7:16

there* and heard how God had put down two of his
enemies who seemed to be the fiercest and most

*Lk 16:8

powerful in their generation.* I am speaking now of
the man at hand and of him whom I mentioned

*See ¶ 23 above

above.* For God overthrew both in an unexpected
way: the one was severely chastised in body, the
other mercifully chastened at heart;[91] both of them

*Ps 10:2

he snared in the counsel they had devised.*

¶27. Once these things had been accomplished the
bishop began to arrange and set in order everything
in the city which pertained to his administration. He
was now entirely free but not without a continual
peril to his own life. For although there was now no
one to harm him openly, there was nevertheless no

place entirely safe from intrigue nor was there any
time when the bishop could relax. Armed men were
assigned to look after him day and night,* though   *Jdt 7:5
he put his trust more readily in the Lord.† Now his   *Ps 11:1, 125:1
plan was to put down the schismatic mentioned
above, because he had been seducing many people*   *Mt 24:5, 11
by the insignia he wore. He succeeded in persuading
everyone that he ought to be bishop and so he was
agitating the people against Malachy and the unity of
the church.[92] He [Malachy] accomplished this,* and   *Is 20:2, Ac 12:8
with no difficulty he so hedged all his ways† by the   †Ho 2:6
grace which was given him by the Lord,* and which   *Rm 12:3, 15:15
he had for all, that the wicked fellow was forced to
throw in his hand, give back the insignia and thereafter hold his peace in subjection.* And so Malachy,   *1 Tm 2:11
despite all these perils and labors, prospered from
day to day and he grew stronger and stronger,
abounding in hope and in the power of the Holy
Spirit.*   *Lk 1:80, Rm
                                                          15:13, Ph 1:9

¶XIII.28. God put down not only those who did
evil to Malachy, but also those who belittled him.
For example: a certain Machprulin[93] who stood well
with the princes and the powerful and even with the
King himself, because he fawned on them and was
loquacious and mighty in tongue,* was well-disposed   *Si 21:8
to all Malachy's enemies in everything and boldly
supported their arguments. When the saint was
present he actually opposed him to his face* and   *Gn 2:11
when he was absent he belittled him. If he met him
anywhere he treated him rudely, especially when he
knew that he was engaged in quite solemn con-
ferences. But soon enough he was given a proper
reward for his pert tongue. His foul tongue swelled
up and putrefied,* and swarming worms issued from   *Ex 16:20
his blasphemous mouth. For seven days he kept
vomiting worms without cease and finally he spewed
out his miserable soul along with them.

¶29. At one time while Malachy was addressing the
people and exhorting them, some miserable woman
dared to break into his homily with indecent shouts,

having no respect for the bishop and the Spirit who
was speaking.* She happened to be of that accursed
race and, having breath in her nostrils,* she vomited
out curses and calumnies against the holy man. She
called him a hypocrite and the usurper of another's
heritage and she even upbraided him for his baldness.
He made no reply to her,* modest and meek as he
was, but the Lord answered for him.† By the judgment of the Lord that woman went mad and kept
crying out that she was being choked by Malachy. In
the end she paid for her sin of blasphemy by a
horrible death. Thus the miserable wretch taking up
against Malachy the reproach that was made to
Elisha found out that he was indeed a second
Elisha.*

¶30. Again, because of some kind of pestilence
which broke out in the city, he solemnly led a crowd
of clergy and people outside with relics of the saints.
Nor must this be glossed over, that the pestilence at
once subsided at Malachy's prayers. And from that
time on there was no one to mutter against him;
those of the seed of Canaan* kept saying: 'Let us flee
Malachy because the Lord fights for him'.* But that
was much too late, for the zeal of the Lord* everywhere engulfed them and pursued them even to
destruction.* How, within a few days, their memory
has perished with the din;* How are they brought to
destruction? They have suddenly ceased to be, they
have perished because of their iniquity.† A great
miracle he performs this day—the speedy annihila-
tion of that generation, especially those who had
known their pride and power. There were many
other signs too* by which God gave glory to His
name and strengthened His servant in his toils and
perils. Who could recount them worthily? Nevertheless we do not pass over them all, even if we are not
up to describing them. But to keep to the thread of
our narrative and not interrupt it we shall reserve for
the end some of the things we shall mention.

¶XIV.31. Once retribution had been made to the

*Ac 6:10
*Jb 27:3, Is 2:22

*Mt 27:12,
  Mk 14:61

†Is 38:14

*2 Kg 2:24

*Dn 13:56
*Ex 14:25
*2 K 19:31

*Dt 7:2
*Ps 9:7

*Ps 73:19

*Jn 20:30

proud,* liberty was restored to the Church, and   *Ps 94:2*
barbarity driven out within three years and the
customs of the christian religion were once more
established. Seeing that everything was at peace,
Malachy began to think of his own peace. Mindful
of his promise he appointed Gelasius[94] to his own
place. He was a good man and worthy of this great
honor, as both clergy and people agreed. I should
rather say they were anxious to keep the pact.*   *See ¶ 21*
have done otherwise would have seemed utterly
harsh. Once he had been consecrated and earnestly
commended to the kings and princes, [Malachy],
famed for his miracles and triumphs, went back to his
own diocese,[95] but not to Connereth. Listen to his
reason, which is worth mentioning here: that diocese
is said to have had two episcopal sees from very early
times and therefore to contain two bishoprics. This
seemed better to Malachy. He re-divided those two
sees which ambition had welded into one, by giving
the one to another bishop and keeping the other for
himself. This was why he did not come to Connereth, because he had already ordained a bishop
there. But he took himself to Down, settling the
diocesan bounds as in the old days.* Oh pure heart!   *Is 51:9*
Oh dove-like eyes![96] He handed over to a new
bishop the place which seemed to be better provided
and was more prestigious, the place in which he himself had been enthroned. Where are those who dispute about boundaries, stirring up endless enmity
among themselves* for a mere village? I know of no   *1 M 7:26, 9:51*
tribe of men to whom the ancient prophecy applies
more than to them: they have ripped up the fertile
lands of Gilead to enlarge their borders.* But more   *Am 1:13*
of this later.

HOW, ONCE INSTALLED AS BISHOP OF
DOWN, HE CONSECRATES EDAN BISHOP
AND SETS OUT FOR ROME. SYCARUS
MAKES A PROPHECY CONCERNING HIM.
HE IS WELL RECEIVED AT CLAIRVAUX.
THEN AT ROME HE RECEIVES THE
OFFICE OF LEGATE OF ALL IRELAND
FROM POPE INNOCENT AND GOES BACK
HOME. MEANWHILE THE ABBEY OF
MELLIFONT IS FOUNDED AND MANY
OTHER THINGS ARE WONDROUSLY
ACCOMPLISHED

¶32. Once Malachy was made Bishop of Down he
immediately concerned himself, as was his custom,
with establishing a convent of regular clerics of his
sons for his solace. Behold, he girds himself again
for the spiritual contest like a new recruit of Christ.
Once again he puts on the weapons so mighty with
Ep 6:10-11   God,* the humility of holy poverty, the rigor of
monastic discipline, the leisure of contemplation and
application to prayer. These were all things which he
had for a long time been able to observe more in
desire than in accomplishment. Indeed everyone
streamed to him in crowds, not only the common
people, but noblemen and those in power. They
rushed to put themselves under his wise direction and
his holiness, to be taught and corrected and to submit to his rule. In the meanwhile he went here and
Lk 8:5   there to sow his seed,* arranging and judging on
ecclesiastical matters with complete authority like
Mt 21:23,   one of the Apostles.[97] And no one said to him:
Mk 11:28   'By what authority do you do these things?'*—
†*Jn 2:23, Ac 8:6*   since they all saw the signs and wonders† which he
2 Cor 3:17   did and because where the Spirit is there is freedom.*

¶XV.33. Nevertheless it seemed to him that one could hardly be engaged in those activities in a safe and satisfactory way without the authority of the Apostolic See and he considered going to Rome—especially because his own metropolitan see lacked (and had from its inception) the use of the *pallium*[98] which is considered the highest mark of honor. It seemed good in his eyes* that the church for which he had struggled so hard should obtain by his endeavors and efforts the right which it had not possessed up till then. There was also another metropolitan see[99] which Cellach had established anew, but subject to the former see and to its archbishop as to a primate. For this see Malachy desired the *pallium* no less, so that the privilege which had been given by Cellach should also have the approval of the Holy See. Once his purpose was made known it displeased the brethren and likewise those in power and all the people of the country.* They all decided that the prolonged absence of their loving father would be intolerable. They also feared for his death.[100]

*1 S 14:36, 40, etc.

*Jn 1:18

¶34. It happened meanwhile that his brother Christian,[101] a good man full of grace and virtue,* died. He was a bishop, second only to Malachy in general esteem, but perhaps not less than he in the holiness of his life and his thirst for justice. It was his death that terrified everyone and rendered even more irksome the departure of Malachy. They said that they would in no way give assent to the pilgrimage of their one and only protector lest the whole country should be more desolate* if it were deprived of two such pillars of strength† at the same time. So they all raised the same objections. And they brought force to bear upon him when he warned them of God's vengeance. They insisted that first God's will in the matter should be ascertained by the casting of lots. This he forbade. Nevertheless they did cast lots, but three times the throw was in Malachy's favor. (They were not satisfied with a single throw, so keen were they to restrain him.) Finally they gave in and allowed him to go, yet not

*Jn 1:14, Ac 6:8, 11:24

*Ezk 12:19, Jr 12:11

†Ps 37:13 (Vulg.)

*Jr 31:15,
Mt 2:18

*Dt 25:5

without weeping and great wailing.* But lest he leave anything undone he began to arrange to bring up the seed of his departed brother.* And when he had summoned three of his disciples, he wavered nervously over which one of them should be more worthy or more useful for this job. Having regarded each of them closely in turn he said: 'You, Edan, (that happened to be the name of one of them) take the burden.' As he hesitated and wept, [Malachy] went on: 'Don't be afraid. You have been pointed out to me by the Lord, for I have just foreseen on your finger the gold ring by which you will be espoused.'[102] He gave his consent and once he had been consecrated, Malachy sets out.

¶35. When, leaving Scotland,[103] he had arrived in York, a certain priest named Sycarus[104] recognized him by looking at him.* For though he had not seen

*Mk 10:21,
Ac 14:8
†Rv 19:10

his face before, since he had the gift of prophecy† things had been revealed about him to Sycarus some time previously. And now he pointed him out unhesitatingly with his finger and said: 'This is the

*Jn 1:30

man of whom I have said,* that from Ireland there shall come a bishop who knows the thoughts of

*Ps 94:11

*Mt 5:15, Mk
4:21, Lk 11:33

men.'* So his lamp could not lie hidden under a bushel while the Holy Spirit who lights it up* made it known through the mouth of Sycarus. Now Sycarus told him many secret things about himself and his companions which he admitted were or had been so. And when Malachy's disciples asked questions about their return, Sycarus answered without hesitation that few of the company would return with

*Gn 41:13

the bishop, and events later proved the truth of this.* When they heard this, they suspected [that their number would be reduced by] death, but God fulfilled it quite differently. For in returning from the city, he left some with us,[105] and others in different places to learn the observances of this way of

*2 K 6:18, etc.

life.[106] According to the word* of Sycarus he did go home to his country with few followers. So much now for Sycarus.

¶36. While Malachy was in the city of York, Waltheof,[107] a man noble by worldly standards, approached him. He was then prior of the regular brothers at Kirkham, but is now a monk and father of the monks at Melrose, a monastery of our own Order. He devoutly, with all humility, commended himself to Malachy's prayers. He referred to the fact that the bishop had many fellow travellers but few horses—for besides servants and other clerics there were five priests with him, but only three horses. He gave him his own horse to ride, saying that he was sorry on one count, namely that it was a rouncy [a pack horse][108] which was hard to ride. And he added: 'I would have given it up more readily if it had been a better animal; but if you are pleased with it take it with you for what it is.'

The bishop answered: 'I accept it more willingly by the very fact that you account it of no worth, for nothing can be worthless to me when it is offered so willingly.' And he turned to his companions and said: 'Prepare this horse for me, because it is just right and will be of service for a long time.' When this was done, he mounted. At first it was rough going, but after a while, by a marvellous change, he found it comfortable and he adjusted himself to the animal's pace. And that nothing of the word which he had spoken* might fall on the ground, that horse never failed him for the nine years until he died. It became a very good and very valuable palfrey.[109] But what was an even greater wonder for those who saw it, the animal from being an almost black color began to become white and pretty soon it was entirely white.[110]

*1 S 3:19,
Mt 10:29

¶XVI.37. I was privileged to see the man Malachy while he was on that journey.* The sight of him and his word renewed me and I was delighted as in all riches.* And I, sinner though I am, found favor in his eyes† from that time until he died, as I have already said in the Preface.[111] He had thought it worthwhile to detour on his journey to visit Clairvaux.[118] Once he had seen the brethren he was deeply impressed

*Ps 32:8,
142:3

*Ps 119:14
†1 S 16:22,
2 S 15:25

and they were greatly edified by his presence and his conversation. Accepting the place and us too and taking us into his inmost heart,[113] he bade us farewell and went on his way. And when he had crossed the Alps he arrived at Iporia,[114] an Italian town, and the first thing he did was to heal the little son of his *Lk 7:2   host who was sick to the point of death.*

¶38. At that time Pope Innocent II of blessed memory occupied the Apostolic See. He received *Ac 28:7   Malachy courteously,* having compassion on him for his lengthy pilgrimage. And first of all, having set his heart firmly on it, Malachy begged with much weeping that he be allowed to live and die at Clairvaux with the permission and blessing of the Supreme Pontiff. He asked this because he had been deeply touched by a yearning for Clairvaux when he had visited, but he was not unmindful of his real purpose in coming. He did not obtain what he asked for, for the Pope judged that he ought to be occupied in more fruitful endeavours.[115] However he was not *Ps 78:30   entirely deprived of his heart's desire,* for it was granted to him at least to die, if not to live, here. He spent a whole month in Rome, making visits to the holy places and coming back to them often for prayer. During that period of time the Supreme Pontiff kept quizzing him and his companions earnestly about their country, the customs of the people, the condition of the churches, and what great things God had done through him in his country. To him, as he was preparing to go back home, the Pope gave his own authority by appointing him legate throughout all Ireland. Bishop Gilbert, whom we mentioned above as having been the Papal Legate, had pointed out to him that because of his age and *Lk 16:2   bodily weakness he could no longer manage things.* After this Malachy asked that the constitution of the *Cashel.   new metropolis* be approved and that *pallia* be See ¶30   given him for both sees. He soon received the privilege of approval, but the Pope told him: 'More formal action must be taken regarding the *pallia*. You are to call together the bishops and clergy and nobles of

your country and hold a general council. Once all the
people agree, you will request the *pallium* through
trustworthy persons and it shall be given to you.'
Then taking the mitre from his own head he placed it
on [Malachy's], but he also gave him the stole and
the maniple which he usually used in the Offering.
Saluting him with the kiss of peace,* he sent him on   *Rm 16:16,
his way supported by the apostolic blessing and   2 Co 13:12
authority.

¶39. Returning by way of Clairvaux, he gave us his
blessing a second time* and he drew deep sighs that   *2 Co 1:15
he was not permitted to remain as he yearned to do.
'These men,' he said, 'I pray that you keep them for
me so that they may learn from you what they may
later teach us.' And he continued: 'They will be seed
to us, and in this seed the people will be blessed,*   *Gn 22:18, 26,4
and those people[116] too who from olden days heard
the word monk, but have never seen a monk.' And
leaving the four who were closest to him,[117] he went
on his way. These men, once tested and found
worthy, became monks. Once the Saint was back in
his own country he sent others* who were treated   *Mt 21:36
likewise.[118] After they had been taught for some
time and were learned in wisdom of heart,* the   *Ps 90:12
saintly brother Christian[119]—who was one of them—
was given to them as father and we sent them out
adding enough of our monks to bring them to the
number of an abbey.[120] [This abbey] conceived and
brought forth five daughter-houses* and so was the   *Gn 4:1, 1 S
seed multiplied† and day by day the number of   2:21, etc.
monks keeps increasing according to the desire and   †Ac 5:14
prophecy[121] of Malachy. But now let us resume the
order of our narrative.

¶XVII.40. Malachy upon leaving us made a good
journey to Scotland. He found King David, who is
still in power, in one of his castles. His son lay sick to
the point of death.* Going into [the king] Malachy   *Jn 4:46, 11:4
was honorably received and humbly entreated to
heal his son.* He blessed water and sprinkled the   *Jn 4:47
youth with it and looking straight at him* said: *Ac 3:4, 13:9

*Mt 9:2

*Jn 21:23
†Mk 7:24

*Is 51:3

*Rm 9:30-31,
  1 Tm 6:11, etc.

*Rm 10:7
†Jn 4:40,
  Ac 10:48

*Mk 7:35

*Lk 19:43

*Mt 4:24

'Have faith, son;* you shall not die this season.' He said this and on the following day the cure followed the word of the prophet; then the joy of the father, the shouting and uproar of the whole exulting household followed the cure. The report spread* to everyone, nor was it possible to keep secret† what had happened in the royal palace and to the king's own son. Thanksgiving and the voice of praise* resounded everywhere for their lord's salvation and the new miracle. This is Henry;[122] he is still alive, the only son of his father, a brave and prudent soldier, taking after his father, as they say, in pursuing justice* and the love of truth. They both loved Malachy as long as he lived because he had called him back from death.* They asked him to remain for some days,† but he, shunning glory, not brooking a delay, took to the road the next morning. As he was passing through the village called Cruggleton,[123] he met with a mute girl. As he prayed the ligament of her tongue was loosed and she spoke clearly.* From there he entered a village which they call the church of Saint Michael[114] and a mad woman bound with cords was brought to him. In front of all of them he cured her and dismissing her, intact, he continued on his journey. But when he came to Port Lapasper[125] his passage was interrupted for some days, though the delay provided very little leisure. During this time he had an oratory built of branches woven into an enclosure.[126] He oversaw the work and helped at it himself. Once it was finished he surrounded it with a wall* and he blessed the enclosed space for a cemetery. Certainly the miracles which they say are performed there even to the present day proclaim well enough the merits of the man who blessed it.[127]

¶41. From then on they used to bring the infirm and the sick from the neighboring region and many are healed.* A woman whose limbs were completely useless was brought there on a cart and she went back home on her own feet, having stayed but a single night in the holy place; not in vain did she look to the mercy of the Lord.

There was another woman who was spending the whole night in prayer* there. A barbarian man, find- *Lk 6:12 ing her all alone and burning with lust and not in the least control of himself, rushed on her in a fit of madness. She turned and trembling she perceived that the man was filled with a diabolical spirit. 'Hey, you,' she said. 'You wretched lout, what are you doing? Consider where you are, respect this holy place, have regard for God, have regard for His servant Malachy and spare yourself.'

He did not stop, impelled by uncontrollable desire.[128] And lo and behold—a horrible thing to speak of—a poisonous bloated animal, a loathsome toad, was seen crawling out from between the woman's thighs. What more can I say? Terrified the man jumped back and with a leap and a bound went out of the oratory at a run. He left utterly routed and she stayed unharmed, thanks to God's miracle and the merits of Malachy. A foul and loathsome monster beautifully prevented a foul and loathsome deed.[129] It is in no way more fitting that animal lust be extinguished than by a slimy worm nor that reckless impetuosity be restrained nor that such intentions be thwarted than by a miserable obnoxious beastie. But here it must suffice to mention only a few of his many [miracles]. Now we shall go on to the rest.

MALACHY'S WAY OF LIFE
AND HIS MIRACLES
ALSO ABOUT THE DEAD
BROUGHT BACK TO LIFE

¶XVIII.42. Malachy boarded ship and after a safe voyage landed at the monastery at Bangor, so that his first sons might receive the first grace.* What attitude do you think they had when they received their father safe after such a long journey—and such a father? It is no wonder they poured out their hearts in sheer joy at his homecoming, whereupon rumor also swiftly spread the unsurpassed joy even to outlaying tribes. From the cities,* from the towns and villages, they came running to him, and whichever way he went he was received with the jubilation of the whole world.* But he does not relish honor. He exercises the office of legate; various assemblies are held in various places so that no region, or part of a region, should be cheated of the fruit and benefit of his legation. He sows over all the waters.* There is no one who may hide himself† from his solicitous care. Neither sex, nor age, nor condition, nor profession makes any difference.[130] Everywhere the health-giving seed is sown, everywhere the heavenly trumpet sounds forth. He keeps rushing about everywhere and he invades everywhere with the sword of his tongue unsheathed to execute vengeance upon the nations, chastisements among the people.* Terror of him is on those who do evil.† He cries out to the wicked: 'Do not act wickedly', and to the sinners: 'lift not up the horn'.*

Religion is planted everywhere, it takes root and it is nursed along. His eyes are on them,* his care is for their needs. In the councils which are being held far and wide they are reviving older traditions which,

*2 Co 1:15

*Mt 9:35,
Lk 13:22

*Ps 48:2

*Is 32:20
†Ps 19:6

*Ps 149:7
†Ps 34:16

*Ps 75:4

*Ps 33:18

although they were considered to have been profitable, had been abolished because of the negligence of the priests. Not only are old [traditions] brought back, but new ones are also being hammered out. Anything that he promulgated is accepted as sent down from heaven; it is kept and committed to writing as a reminder to posterity. And why shouldn't these things be considered as heaven-sent, when so many heavenly miracles ratified them? And in order to confirm what has been said, let me briefly relate a few of them. Who could even count all of them? I admit that I'd rather dwell upon things worth imitating than on those worth marvelling at.

¶XIX.43. In my opinion, the first and the greatest miracle that he presented was the man himself.[131] I do not even mention the inner man.* His life and way of life showed forth his beauty and courage and purity, and he carried himself outwardly in so modest and becoming a manner that there was nothing in him which could displease those who saw him. And anyone who offends not in word is a perfect man.* And no one who watched Malachy, no matter how closely, ever caught him using an idle word* or even, I tell you, a nod. Who ever saw him using either his hand or his foot to no purpose? Was there anything in his walk, his appearance, his bearing, or his countenance that was not edifying? I might add that sadness did not darken the joyousness of his countenance, nor did a smile turn it to lightheadedness.[132] He kept himself under strict discipline, totally marked with virtue, the model of perfection.[133] In everything he was serious without being austere. At times he was relaxed but never dissipated. He neglected nothing, even if for a time he paid no attention to many things. He was often quiet, but almost never idle. From the first day of his conversion to the end of his life he lived with nothing his own. He had no man-servants, no maid-servants,* no villages, no hamlets not even any sort of revenue either ecclesiastical or secular, even when he was a bishop. Nothing was appropriated or assigned to his

*Rm 7:22,
Eph 3:16*

Jm 3:2

Mt 12:36

Gn 32:5

episcopal upkeep from which the bishop might live.
Nor did he even have a house of his own. He was continually going about all the dioceses[134] both serving

*1 Co 9:14
†Lk 10:7

the Gospel and living the Gospel* as the Lord had
ordered saying: 'The worker is worthy of his hire.'†
But more frequently he was delivering the same

*1 Cor 9:18,
Bernard,
Serm 2:1

Gospel without charge,* making by his own labors
and those of his disciples something by which he
could support himself and those who worked with

*Ph 4:3; Ep 4:12,
cf. Ac 20:34

him in the work of the ministry.* Furthermore, if it
was necessary for him to seek rest now and again,
he did so in holy places which he himself had spread
all over Ireland. At places where he was pleased to
make a stopover, he adapted himself to the customs
and observances of the place, content with the common way of life and table. There was nothing in his
food or in his apparel by which Malachy could be
distinguished from the other brothers. This he carried

*Mt 18:4, see
Si 3:20

to such a degree that although he was greater he
humbled himself in all things.*

¶44.   Then when he went out preaching he went on
foot along with companions on foot, he the bishop
and legate. This is the apostolic model and therefore
the more wonderful in Malachy as it is extremely rare
in others. Truly he who does such things is the true
heir of the Apostles. But it is worth observing how
he would divide the inheritance with his own

*Lk 12:13
*1 P 5:3

brothers* who are equally the kinsmen of the
Apostles. They lorded it over the clergy;* he,
whereas he was free from all men, made himself the

*1 Co 9:19

servant of all.* They either eat without preaching the
Gospel or they preach the Gospel so that they may
eat; Malachy, imitating Saint Paul, eats in order to
preach the Gospel.[135] They think that haughtiness

*1 Tm 6:5

and profit are godliness;* Malachy claims labor and a
burden for himself by hereditary right. They believe

*Ex 34:24,
Am 1:13
†2 Co 6:11
*Mt 6:23

themselves fortunate if they enlarge their boundaries;*
Malachy takes glory in enlarging his charity.† They
gather into barns* and fill their jars to load down
their tables; Malachy brings men together into deserts
and solitudes that he may people heaven. Although

receive tithes and first-fruits and oblations,*   *Nb 18:26-27
not to mention customs and tribute from Caesar's
benefice and other revenues too numerous to mention, they are still anxious about what they shall eat
and what they will drink;* having none of these   *Mt 6:25
Malachy still enriches many† from the storehouse   †2 Co 6:10
of faith. There is no end to their covetousness and
their anxiety; desiring nothing, does not
even know how to take thought for tomorrow.*   *Mt 6:24
They exact from the poor payment that they give
to the wealthy; he exhorts the rich to help the poor.
They empty the purses of their subjects; he loads the
altars[136] with vows and peace offerings for their
sins.* They erect lofty palaces and raise towers and   *Nb 29:39
walls to the heavens;* Malachy having no place to lay   *Gn 11:4
his head,* does the work of an evangelist.† They ride   *Mt 8:20, Lk 9:58
horseback** with a crowd of men who eat bread for   †2 Tm 4:5
doing nought, and that not their own;† Malachy   **Jr 6:23
surrounded by a congregation of holy brethren, goes   †2 Th 3:8,12
around on foot, carrying the bread of angels* with   *Ps 78:25
which he will satisfy hungry souls.† They do not   †Ps 107:9
even recognize their parishoners;[137] he instructs
them. They honor men of power and tyrants; he cas-
tigates them. Oh apostolic man, whom so many and
such great signs of his apostolate have ennobled!*   *2 Co 12:12
Why then should we wonder if he has done wondrous
deeds, seeing that he is himself so wonderful?[138] Yet
it is not he, but God in him.* Besides there is a say-   *1 Co 15:10
ing: You are the God who works wonders.*   *Ps 77:14

¶XX.45. There was a woman in the city of Coleraine[139] afflicted with a demon.[140] Malachy was
called; he prays for the possessed woman and bears
down upon the Invader. It left her but its malice was
not yet fully glutted and it entered into a miserable
wretch of a woman who happened to be standing
nearby. Malachy spoke out: 'I did not free that
woman from your clutches so you would enter this
one. Get out of her at once.'* It obeyed, but went   *Mk 9:24
back to the first woman. When it had been driven
out again it ran back to the other woman. This went
on for quite a time, bothering them in turns and thus

*Jn 11:34

keeping safe. Then the saint became angry at being
thwarted by a demon and he concentrated his spirit
and bellowed out.* And bringing to bear all the forces
of faith against the Adversary, he drove it out from
both women, no less agitated than the women it had
vexed. Now do not imagine, reader, that the delay was
caused for the saint by [the demon's] own strength;
it happened by divine plan so that its evil presence,
and Malachy's victory, should be more manifest.
Listen now to what he accomplished in other places,
not because he was present. Certainly what he could
do when present he was also able to do when absent.

*Mt 8:6

¶46. In the district of Li[141] in the northern part of
Ireland lay a sick man* at home and there was no
doubt it was because of the evil doings of demons. He
actually heard them talking one night, the one saying
to the other: 'Look out lest that miserable man touch
the bed or the quilts of that hypocrite and so escape

*2 Co 11:33

our clutches.'* The man realized that they were
referring to Malachy, who he remembered had spent
the night in that very house not long before. Now his
bedding was still in place. Summoning courage and
making every effort he could, the sick man began to
creep toward [the bed], weak in body but strong in

*1 P 5:9

faith.* And suddenly an outcry and clamor rent the
air: 'Stop him! Stop! hold him, grab him, we are
losing our prey!' But he was carried along by faith and
the desire to escape, and the more the cry went up,
the more he hastened toward the remedy, crawling on
his hands and knees. Reaching the bed, he climbed in,
he rolled himself up in the bed-clothes and he heard
the howls of the lamenting demons: 'Alas! Alack! we
gave ourselves away, we have been cheated. He got
away!' And quicker than it takes to say it, the terror
of the demons and the horror he had suffered left
him, as well as all his sickness.[142]

In the city of Lismore a man vexed by a demon
was freed by Malachy. On another occasion as he was
passing through Leinster a young child having a
demon was brought to him and was taken back
cured. In the same region he ordered a lunatic woman

who had been bound with straps to be freed and washed in water which he had blessed. She was washed and she was cured.[143]

In a region of Ulidia[144] at Saul there was another woman whom he cured by prayer and touching her. She had been biting her own limbs with her teeth. Relatives and neighbors brought to the man of God a madman who foretold many future events. He was bound tightly with cords because his frenzies made him dangerous and terribly strong. Malachy prays over him and at once the sick man is healed and unbound. This happened in a certain place whose name we will not mention* because it has a barbarous sound, like so many others. Another time in the afore-mentioned city of Lismore her parents brought a mute girl[145] to him as he passed down the middle of the street and they implored him with many entreaties to deign to come to their aid. Malachy stopped and having said a prayer and touching her tongue with his finger, he put spittle* on her mouth and he sent her away speaking.

Whether this was a literary device or a linguistic difficulty in pronouncing an Irish name, we cannot be certain. Saint Gregory, the Venerable Bede, Jocelin, and others characterized the Celtic languages as barbarous, since they contained sounds not known to classical writers.

*Mk 7:33

¶XXI.47. As he was leaving a certain church he met a man with his wife who was unable to speak. Asked to have pity on her, he stood at the gate and, with all the folk standing around him, he gave her a blessing and commanded her to say the Lord's Prayer. She said it and the people praised the Lord. In the city called Antrim[146] there was a man lying in bed who had been deprived of the use of his tongue now for twelve days. At the command of the saint who visited him, he recovered his speech and took the Eucharist and thus fortified he breathed out his last breath in a good confession.* Oh fruitful olive tree† in the house of God! Oh oil of gladness* anointing and enlightening! By the splendor of a miracle he gave light to the healthy and by the sweetness of a favor he anointed the sick man for whom, at the point of death, he obtained the saving ability of confessing and making communion.[147]

*1 Tm 6:13
†Ps 52:8
*Ps 45:7

One of the nobles came to see him having something to say to him.* While the conversation was

*Lk 7:40

*Ac 6:5

going on, being full of faith* he piously stole three
rushes from the couch where he was sitting
and he took them away with him. • And
God did many good works from this pious theft, by
the man's faith and the holiness of the bishop. Quite
by chance he came to the city called Cloyne.[148] While
he was seated at the table a nobleman of that city
came in and humbly entreated him on the behalf of
his pregnant wife who had passed the usual time for
giving birth so far that everyone was astonished.
There was no one who did not believe that she was
running a risk to her life. Nehemiah,[149] the bishop of
that city who sat next to him, also made the same
request as did others who were reclining together.
Then [Malachy] said: 'I take pity on her for she is a
good and modest woman.' Holding out to the man a
cup which he had blessed, he said, 'Go, give her this to
drink; know that once she takes the blessed drink she
will give birth without delay or rush.' It was done as
he commanded and that very night what he had
promised came to pass.[150]

*Lk 6:17

He was seated on the plain with the count[151] of
the Ulidians discussing some matters and there was a
great throng* around them. There came a pregnant
woman and she was very pregnant. She declared that
against all the laws of nature she had carried the
baby for fifteen months and twenty days. With
compassion for this strange and unheard of misfortune, Malachy prayed and the woman gave birth.
Everyone there was happy and marvelled at it. For
they all saw the ease and speed with which she gave
birth in that very place. Thus the sad wonder of a
birth denied was changed into a more joyful wonder.

¶XXII.48. In the same place there occurred something in a similar miracle, but of a different kind. He
noticed a man who was said to carry on openly with
his brother's concubine, and he was a knight, a
servant of the count.[152] When he met that incestuous
man publicly he showed himself another John, saying:

*Mk 6:18
(Vulg.
ux orem)

'It is not lawful for you to have your brother's concubine.'* But he showed himself to [Malachy] no less

another Herod; not only did he not heed him, but he replied haughtily and he swore before everyone* that he would never send her away. Then Malachy, as deeply moved as he was vehemently zealous for justice, said: 'And may God separate you from her whether you choose or not.' Paying little attention to this, he went off at once in a huff. Meeting up with the woman not far from the crowd gathered there, he forcibly violated her as if he were Satan's own, to whom he had shortly before been committed.* Nor was the disgraceful act hidden: a maid-servant who had gone along with her mistress rushed back to the house—for it was not too far from the place—and breathlessly reported the evil that was taking place.

*Mk 6:26

*1 Co 5:5,
 1 Tm 1:20

On hearing this her brothers who were at home, eager to avenge the foul deed, rushed there quickly and killed that enemy of modesty, caught in the very place and act of the crime,* and they riddled his body with many wounds. The assembly had not yet broken up when his squire announced what had happened. They all marvelled* that Malachy's pronouncement should have had so quick an effect. When word got around, the evildoers—and there were many in the land—all took fright and purged themselves, washing their hands in the blood of the sinner.*

*Jn 8:4

*Lk 1:63

*Ps 58:10

¶XXIII.49. Dermot[153] the count had been bedridden for a long time. Malachy chastised him harshly because he was a bad fellow immoderately serving his belly* and his gullet. He sprinkled him with holy water and made him get up without delay, and he was well enough to mount his horse at once—something that neither he nor his followers had even hoped for. In the town of Cashel a man came to him with a son who was a paralytic* and asked that he be cured.[154] Saying a short prayer [Malachy] said: 'Go your way; your son will be cured.'* He did go and he returned the following day with his son, but he was only partially cured. Then Malachy, getting up and standing over him, prayed for quite a long time and he was cured. Turning to the father he said: 'Offer

*Rm 16:18

*Mt 8:6, Jn 4:47

*Mt 8:13, Jn 4:50

him to God.'[155] The man gave, but did not hold to, his promise and after some years that boy, now a young man, relapsed into the same condition. There is no doubt that this was because of the father's disobedience and his breaking of the promise. Another man, coming from afar* while Malachy was in the borders of Munster, brought him his son who was completely deprived of the use of his feet. Being asked how this had happened, he replied: 'I suppose it was by the evil work of demons.' Then he added: 'Unless I am mistaken, they caused a sleep to come over him* as he was playing in a field and when the little fellow woke up he found himself in this condition.' Saying this he poured forth his petition with tears and he demanded help. Filled with pity for him Malachy prayed and he bade the sick boy sleep there on the ground. He slept and arose completely cured. Since he had come from afar off* [Malachy] kept him for a while in his company and he used to walk with him.

¶50. In the monastery at Bangor there was a certain poor man who was kept alive by the alms of the brethren. Every day he received a small coin for doing some sort of work in the mill. He had been lame for twelve years, crawling along on the ground with his hands and dragging his lifeless feet behind him. Malachy discovered him one day in front of his cell, sad and mournful, and he inquired the cause. 'You see,' said he, 'how poor miserable me am afflicted for so long and the hand of the Lord is on me.* And look here, to add to my misfortune, men who should have shown pity make fun of me instead and reproach my misery.' Moved with pity when he heard him, Malachy looked up to heaven,* raising his hands at the same time. Having said a short prayer, he went into his cell and the crippled man got up. And as he stood on his feet* he wondered if it were true, almost suspicious that it was a dream.† Yet he began to move step by step, not really believing that he could walk. Finally, as if awakening out of a deep sleep,* he recognized the mercy of the Lord† upon him. He

Is 30:27, Mk 8:3

Gen 2:21

Is 30:27, Mk 8:3

Ac 13:11

Mk 7:34

Ac 26:16
†Ac 12:9

Gn 45:26
†Si 18:12

strode along steadily and went back to the mill leaping and exultant, praising God.* Those who had seen him and known him before were filled with wonder and amazement† at seeing him, thinking it a mirage.* He likewise cured a man suffering from dropsy by praying. He stayed there in the monastery and was made shepherd of the flock.

*Ac 3:8

†Ac 3:10
*Mk 6:49:
 phantasma

¶51. A city of Ireland called Cork[156] was without a bishop. An election was called but the parties could not agree; as often happens each side had its own prelate in mind, not God's. When Malachy heard about the argument he came there. Having called together the clergy and the people, he made every attempt to bring into one the hearts and choice of the people. Once he had persuaded them that they should leave the entire decision to him since the special care of this as well as of the other churches* throughout Ireland was especially incumbent on him, he named a candidate for them without delay. It was not one of the nobles of the country but rather a poor man whom he knew to be both learned and holy and he happened to be an outsider.[157] They sought him out, but he was reported to be lying abed and so weak that he could leave only if he were carried in the arms of his attendants. Malachy spoke up: 'Let him arise in the name of the Lord.* I tell you, obedience will make him whole.' What would he do? He was willing to obey, but he felt that even if he could go he was wholly unprepared and he dreaded being made a bishop. So along with the desire to obey there were twin enemies facing him: the weight of his weariness and the fear of the burden. But obedience won out; the hope of salvation was given to help him.* So he tried, he moved, he tested his strength and found that he was stronger than usual. His faith increased with his strength and once faith became stronger in turn, it gave increase to his strength. He was now able to get up by himself and to walk a little better and he did not tire himself out by walking. Finally he was able to come to Malachy without hindrance and quickly, without

*2 Co 11:28

*Ac 3:6

*Ps 93:22 (Vulg.)

everyone's help. Malachy took him in hand and enthroned him amid the applause of clergy and people. This was done peaceably, for no one dared to oppose the will of Malachy in any way after seeing

Jn 2:23, 6:14   the sign he had done.* Nor did the other man hesitate to obey since by so clear a proof he was quite certain of God's will.

¶52. A certain woman was troubled with an issue of blood*[158] and she was a noble woman, very dear to Malachy, noble in her way of life rather than by birth.

Mk 5:23   She was rapidly failing and close to the end,* all her strength drained away with her blood. She sent for the man of God, not so much for the sake of her body, as he would never see her alive, but to succor her soul. Malachy worried when he heard this because she was a virtuous woman and her life abounded in work and example. Perceiving that he could not reach her in time, he sent for Malchus because he was young and swift of foot. Actually, he is the one we mentioned before, the brother of Christian the

See ¶14.   abbot.* 'Hurry,' he said, 'take her these three apples
†2 S 6:2,   over which I called upon the name of the Lord.† I
Ps 116:4   have complete confidence that once she has tasted these she shall not taste death before she sees me,*
*Mk 16:28,   even though I shall come somewhat later.' Malchus
Mk 8:39,   hurried as commanded and when he arrived he went
Lk 9:27   in to the dying woman, showing himself another servant of Elisha except that his offering was more

2 K 4:29-36   effectual.* He commanded her to take what Malachy had blessed and to taste them if she possibly could. Now she was so delighted when she heard Malachy's name mentioned that she could obey and by a sign she indicated that she was willing to be raised up for a short while (for she could not speak). She was raised up, tasted [the apples] and drew strength from that taste and she spoke, and gave thanks. And the Lord

Gn 2:21   cast a deep sleep upon her* and she rested sweetly in it, having lacked sleep as well as food for a long

Lk 8:44   time. Meanwhile the blood stopped flowing* and when, after a short while, she was aroused she found

Mk 5:29   herself well,* except that she was still weak from the

long fast and loss of blood. Anything less than perfect
health the anticipated coming and sight of Malachy
the next day made up for.

¶XXIV.53. In the neighborhood of the monastery
of Bangor lived a nobleman whose wife was sick to
the point of death.* Malachy was begged to come   *Ph 2:27
down before she died,† to anoint her with oil.** He   †Jn 4:47, 11:4
came down and went in to her. She rejoiced at seeing   **Jm 5:14
him, enlivened by the hope of health. And although
he was getting ready to anoint her, everyone thought
it were better to defer it until morning (it was even-
ing). Malachy agreed and after blessing the sick
woman he left with those who were with him. But a
little while later there was suddenly a cry,* weeping   *Mt 25:6
and great commotion throughout the house, because
it was reported that she had died. Malachy came
running when he heard the noise and his disciples   *Mt 8:23
followed him. And approaching the bed to ascertain
that she had really died, Malachy was greatly per-
turbed in mind, blaming himself that she had passed
away deprived of the grace of the Sacrament. Raising
his hands to heaven, he said: 'I beseech you, O Lord,
I have acted foolishly.* I, it is I who have sinned;†   *1 Ch 21:8
I who deferred [giving the Sacrament], it is not she,   †2 S 24:17
she desired it.' This is what he said and he claimed in
everyone's hearing that he would take no comfort*   *Gn 37:35
or give any rest to his spirit,† unless he were allowed   †2 Co 2:13
to restore the grace which he had removed. He stood
over her and he agonized, groaning all night, and
instead of holy oil he kept pouring a great flood of
tears* over the dead woman, giving her that in place   *Ps 6:6
of holy unction. Then he spoke thus to his disciples:
'Watch and pray.'* So they kept the night vigil with   *Mk 26:41
psalms; he with tears. Come morning the Lord heard
his servant because the Spirit of the Lord was begging
on his behalf, who intercedes for the saints with
unspeakable groanings.* Why say more? The woman   *Rm 8:26
who had been dead opened her eyes,† and rubbing   †Ac 9:40
her forehead and temples with her hands, as those do
who awaken from a deep sleep,* she got up from   *Si 22:8
her cough and, recognizing Malachy, she bowed

devoutly and greeted him. And as their sorrow
turned into joy;* they were all astonished,† both
those who saw it and those who heard of it.
Malachy too gave thanks, blessing the Lord. And he
anointed her* nevertheless, knowing that in this
sacrament sins are forgiven and that the prayer of
faith saves the sick.† After this he went off and she
completely recovered. When she had continued for
some time in good health, so that the glory of the
Lord should be made manifest in her,* she performed
the penance which Malachy had imposed upon her.
Then once more she fell asleep† in a good confession*
and went to the Lord.

¶XXV.54. Then too there was a woman whom a
spirit of temper and fury* so dominated that not only
did her neighbors and kinsfolk flee her company, but
even her own offspring could hardly bear to live with
her. Wherever she happened to be there was shouting
and rancor and a mighty uproar.† She was foolhardy,
outrageous, and quick-tempered, formidable in both
tongue and hand, impossible to live with and despised.
Her offspring ached for her, as well as for themselves,
and they dragged her into the presence of Malachy,
explaining their sad situation amid weeping. The
holy man took pity both on the mother's sad condition and on her offsprings' troubles. Calling her aside,
he carefully inquired whether she had ever confessed
her sins. 'Never,' she replied. 'Confess,' he told her.
She obeyed. Then he assigned a penance to her when
she confessed and over her he prayed* that the Lord
Almighty should give her the spirit of meekness† and
in the name of the Lord Jesus he commanded her
never to lose her temper again. Such great meekness
followed that it was clear to everyone that this was
nothing other than a miraculous change [brought
about] by the right hand of the Most High.* They say
that she is still alive today and exercises such patience
and gentleness that whereas she used to exasperate
everyone she is now never exasperated by any
injuries or abuses or torments. Should even I be
allowed, according to the Apostle, to attach my own

*Est 13:17,
 Jn 16:20
†Lk 5:26

*Jm 5:14

†Jm 5:15

*Jn 2:11, 9:3

†Ac 7:59
*1 Tm 6:13

*Ex 15:8

*Ps 50:3

*Jm 5:14
†1 Co 4:21

*Ps 77:10

meaning.* Then let each person take this as he will.
I am of the opinion that this is to be put ahead of the
miracle of raising up the dead woman mentioned
above. The former was an exterior act, but here the
inner person* was brought back to life. But now let
us hasten on to others.

Rm 14:5

Eph 3:16,
2 Co 4:16

¶55. A man honorable by worldly standards and by
God's God-fearing* came to Malachy and complained of the dryness of his soul.† He entreated him
to obtain for him from Almighty God the gift of
tears. Malachy smiled, gratified to learn that there
should be spiritual yearnings in a man of the world.
He laid his cheek on the other's cheek, as if joining
him in a caress and said: 'May it happen for you as
you have asked.'* From then on rivers of waters
ran down his eyes;† such great rivers and so nearly
continual that it would seem there could be applied
to him that saying of Scripture: the fountain of the
gardens, the well of living waters.*

There is in the sea near Ireland an island very
productive of fish from olden times and the sea there
abounds in fish.[159] This usual great supply of fish disappeared, because (they thought) of the sins of the
islanders. She that had many children was
weakened* and her great usefulness all but dried up.
While the woeful islanders and all the people greatly
bemoaned this misfortune, it was revealed to some
woman that a remedy might be effected by the
prayers of Malachy. She kept mentioning this and
soon everyone knew of it.* By God's will Malachy
happened by. While going about filling the country
with the Gospel, he made a detour there to impart
the same grace to them.* But the barbarians,† more
interested in fish, importuned him earnestly to pay
attention instead to the barrenness of their island. He
replied that he had not come for that purpose, that it
was men he wished to catch rather than fish.*
Nevertheless he saw their faith† and kneeling down
on the shore* he prayed to the Lord† that although
the people were unworthy, He should not deny to a
people who begged it with such great faith the

Lk 2:25
†Ps 35:12

Mt 8:13,
Jn 15:7

†Ps 119:136

Sg 4:15

1 S 2:5

Ac 1:19

Rm 1:11
†Ac 28:1

Lk 5:10
†Mk 2:5
Ac 21:5
†2 K 4:33

*Ac 10:4

†Lk 5:6, Jn 21:6

*Si 35:21

†Ps 107:27

benefit of old. The prayer went up* and there also came up a multitude of fish,† and perhaps even more abundant than in the old days and it continues for the folk of that land to the present day. Why wonder if the prayer of the just man which pierces the heavens* has pierced the depths of the sea† and from there has called forth an abundance of fish?

¶56. Once three bishops came to the village of Faughart,[160] which they claim is the birthplace of Brigid the virgin,[161] and the fourth bishop was Malachy. The priest who had taken them into his lodging said to him: 'What shall I do? I have no fish.' [Malachy] replied that he should ask among the fishermen. 'It is now two years since any fish have been found in the river,'[162] he replied, 'and for that reason the fishermen are completely disillusioned and have given up their art.' But [Malachy] said: 'Command *Lk 5:4 them to let down their nets* in the Lord's name.' They did so and caught twelve salmon. They cast them a second time and caught just as many. To the tables they brought an unexpected dish and a miracle as well. And to make it clear that this was granted to the merits of Malachy, the same lack of fish nevertheless continued for the following two years.

HOW A CLERIC DID NOT BELIEVE THAT
THE TRUE BODY WAS PRESENT IN THE
SACRAMENT OF THE ALTAR WAS RE-
PROACHED AND SIMILAR HOPELESS
FOLK WERE REFORMED
BY SAINT MALACHY

¶57. There was a certain cleric in Lismore, good in his character, they say, but not in his faith. In his own eyes a knowledgeable man,[163] he had the presumption to say that in the Eucharist there is only a sacrament and not the *res sacramenti,* that it is only the sanctification and not the true presence of the Body.[164] He had often been called up on this by Malachy in secret, but to no purpose. Then he was summoned into the open and the lay people were excluded, so that if it were possible, he could be cured of this malady rather than be confuted. So it was that in an assembly of clerics the man was given the opportunity to defend his own viewpoint. Although he attempted to set forth and defend his error with every power of ingenuity—which he was not unskilled in, with Malachy arguing against and refuting him, he was worsted in everyone's opinion. He left the assembly confuted but not corrected. He said however that he was not conquered by reasoning, but crushed by the bishop's authority. 'And you, Malachy!' he said, 'have confuted me without good reason today, speaking against the truth and against your own conscience.'

Malachy, saddened for so hardened a man, but sorrowing even more for the injury to the faith and fearing the danger, convoked the church and publicly scolded* the erring man and advised him publicly to come to his senses. The bishop and all the clergy kept persuading him. When still he did not submit, they   *Lv 19:17* pronounced an anathema on this stubborn man, publicly declaring him a heretic. Still he did not come to his senses. 'All of you curry favor with one man,' he said, 'instead of considering the truth. I shall not accept this person and so desert the truth.'* The saint was not a little peeved[165] at this and said: 'May the Lord force you to tell the truth.' And when he replied 'Amen', the meeting broke up.

Pr 28:21

Branded as he was with such an iron, he considered flight, being unable to bear disesteem and dishonor. So he gathered up his things and made off when he was taken with a sudden weakness. He stopped in his tracks and, losing all his strength, he sank to the ground gasping for breath and worn out. A mad vagabond happening along came upon the man and asked him what he was doing there. He replied that he was seized by a great weakness and could go neither backwards nor forwards. The madman replied: 'This weakness is nothing but the warning of death.' This he spoke not of himself* but through the madman God was reprimanding him in a beautiful way, since he had gained nothing from the sane counsels of sensible men. And he added: 'Go back home. I'll help you.' Finally, led by [the vagabond], he went back to the city. He also made a return to the heart* and to the mercy of God. Within the hour the bishop was called, truth was acknowledged and error rooted out. He confessed that he had been in the wrong and was absolved. Then he asked for the *Viaticum* and a reconciliation was effected. At practically the same moment that his lips renounced all his faithless wrong-doing he was dissolved by death. And so as they all marvelled at it, the word of Malachy was speedily accomplished and likewise that of Scripture which says that distress gives understanding to the hearing.*

Jn 11:51

Is 46:8

Is 28:19

¶XXVII.58. At another time serious discord arose among the peoples of certain regions.[166] Malachy was besought to bring about peace between them,* but since he was hindered by other affairs he assigned this business to one of his [suffragan] bishops. He

1 M 9:70

begged off on the grounds that Malachy was the one
who was sought and not himself, that he would only
be held in contempt and he was unwilling to go to all
that trouble in vain. 'Go,' said Malachy, 'and the
Lord will be with you.'* And he replied: 'All right,
but if they will not listen to me, you must realize
that I shall make an appeal to your fatherhood.[167]
Malachy smiled and said: 'That may be so.'

*1 S 17:37,
1 Ch 22:16

Then the bishop called the parties together and
dictated the terms of peace. They agreed and were
reconciled to each other, each giving proper security.
Peace was established and he sent them away. But the
one party, realizing that its enemy was rendered
careless and therefore unprepared, since they suspected no evil once peace was made, conferred among
themselves, each man to his neighbor:* 'What were
we trying to do? Victory and revenge over our
enemy* is in our hands.' And they began to harass
them. The bishop became aware of it and went to
meet their leader in regard to their wickedness and
treachery,* but he was scorned by him. He appealed
to him in Malachy's name, but he paid him no heed.
Laughing at the bishop he said: 'Do you think that
for you we ought to let these men go who did evil
to us when God has delivered them into our hands?'*
And the bishop, calling to mind his own words
which he had had with Malachy, weeping and wailing,* turned his face towards his monastery and
said: 'Where are you, man of God? Where are you?
Is this not, father of mine, what I told you? Alas,
alas! I came to do good and not evil* and look, they
are all perishing on my account, some in the body,
others in the soul.' He kept talking this way,
mourning and lamenting* and he begged and urged
Malachy against the evil-doers* as though he were
present. Meanwhile the impious men did not stop
attacking those with whom they had made peace,
intending to kill them. And behold there was
in the mouth of some men a lying spirit to deceive
them.* On the way men met them and announced
that an invasion into their lands had been made by
their adversaries, that everything had been destroyed

*Gn 11:3

*1 S 18:25

*Ws 1:9

*Jg 3:28, 16:24

*Mk 5:38

*Pr 31:12

*Mt 11:17
*Ps 94:16

*1 K 22:22,
2 Ch 18:21

*Nb 21:24
†Est 3:13

*Heb 11:8

*1 Jn 4:6

*Ml 1:6

by the edge of the sword,* that their property had
been plundered† and that their wives and children
had been seized and taken away. When they heard
this they beat a hasty retreat. The last followed the
first, not knowing where they were going* or what
was happening. Not everyone had heard the men who
spoke. When they arrived and found nothing of what
had been announced they were confused, caught up
in their own wickedness. And they knew that they
had been betrayed to the spirit of error* because they
had deceived Malachy's messenger and spurned his
name.* Afterwards the bishop, hearing that the
traitors were disappointed in the iniquity they had
planned, went back to Malachy joyfully and related
in order everything that had happened to him.

¶59. Malachy, realizing that the peace is disturbed
by such occasions and finding an opportune time,
concerned himself with restoring peace again by his
own efforts and at once it was restored by confirming
it by a granting and receiving of security and oath
binding upon both parties. Nevertheless those whose
peace had been broken were mindful of the injury
and with no regard for the pledge or Malachy's command prepared to take vengeance. Gathering to-

*Jn 11:52

gether,* they went to take their unprepared enemy
by surprise, to bring down on their own head the evil
which the enemy had planned to do to them. A great
river lay between them which they had forded very
easily, but they were held back by a small stream
which they encountered not far away. But now it was
not merely a small stream but seemed to be a great
river, everywhere blocking the passage of those who
wished to cross. Everyone marvelled at its great size,
knowing full well that it had been very small before,
and they said to one another: 'Whence this flooding?
The air is clear, there are no storms, nor do we remember any recent one. Even if it had rained a lot,
who of us remembers it ever flooding so much that it
covered the land, the sown fields and the meadows?

*Ex 8:19

This is the finger of God* and the Lord is hedging our
ways because of his holy Malachy whose command

we have transgressed* and side-stepped his pact.'†
And so they too, without finishing their business,
retreated to their territory equally confused. The
word spread around through the entire region* and
they blessed God who caught the wise in their own
craftiness* and, cutting off the horns of the wicked,†
exalted the horn of his anointed.**

*Jos 7:15
†cf. Passing 2:2

*Mt 28:15,
  Lk 4:14
*1 Co 3:19
†Ps 75:10
**1 S 2:10

¶60. One of the nobles hostile to the king was
reconciled by Malachy's hand. For he did not trust
the king enough to make peace with him unless the
arbiter were Malachy or someone else whom the
king held in equal reverence. This was not without
reason as was only too clear afterwards. The king
captured him, become careless and heedless of his
safety, and put him in chains, really himself captured
by the old hatred. The man was asked for by his
people from the hand of the arbiter;* they expected
no more for their friend than death. What would
Malachy do? There was nothing he could do except
go back to the usual refuge of his. He gathered up a
mighty strong army*—a great throng of his own
disciples—and going to the king he asked for the
bound man. He was refused. And Malachy said:
'You are acting unfairly, against the Lord, against me
and against yourself in transgressing the covenant.*
If you misrepresent it, I shall not. The man entrusted
himself to my guarantee. If he should die, I have
betrayed him and I am guilty of his blood.* What do
you think made me a traitor and yourself a perjuror?
You should realize that I will eat nothing until† he is
freed; nor will these [my companions].'¹⁶⁸ Having
said this, he entered the church. With his groanings
and those of his companions he beseeched Almighty
God that He should deem worthy of delivery out of
the hand of the transgressor and unjust man* the one
who had been unjustly apprehended. And they persisted in fasting and prayer* that day and the following night. The king was informed of what was
happening, but his heart was even more hardened*
when it should have been softened. The carnal man
took flight, fearing that should he remain close by

*Gal 3:19

*1 M 1:14

*Josh 7:15

*Ex 22:2,
  Lv 17:4
†Ac 23:14

*Ps 71:4, 82:4

*Tb 3:11

*Ex 7:13, 8:19

he would not be able to withstand the power of
prayer—as if it would not find him if he hid himself or
could not penetrate to far-off places! Would you hem
Rv 5:8, 8:3   in the prayers of the saints, wretched man?* Is
prayer an arrow shot forth, that you may flee from
Ps 60:4, Is 21:15   the face of the bow?* Where will you go from the
Spirit of God who carries it, and where will you flee
Ps 139:7   from his face?* Finally [Malachy] pursued the fugi-
tive and he found him hiding away:
Ac 13:11   'You shall be blind and not seeing* so that you
may see and understand the better, for it is hard for
Ac 9:5   you to kick against the goad.* Sense, even now, that
†*Ps 120:4*   the sharp arrows of the mighty† have reached you.
They have ricocheted from your stony heart, yet not
from your eyes. If only they would reach your heart
through the windows of your eyes and vexation
Is 28:19   would give understanding* to your blindness.'
Ac 9:8-18   It was seeing Saul being taken by the hand* again
and led to Ananias, the wolf to the sheep, as it were,
that he might return his booty. He disgorged it and
Ac 9:18   received his sight* because were Malachy the sheep
up to this point he would have pity even on the wolf.
From this, reader, note carefully what sort of princes
and peoples Malachy lived among. How was it that he
was not also a brother of dragons and companion of
Jb 30:29   ostriches?* And therefore the Lord gave him the
Lk 10:19   power to tread upon serpents and scorpions,* to
bind their kings in fetters and their nobles with
Ps 149:8   manacles of iron.* Hear now the sequel.

THE PROPHECY OF THE STONE ORATORY,
THE FIRST BUILT IN THAT LAND, AND
THE TROVE TREASURE

¶XXVIII.61. The man to whom Malachy had sur-
rendered the possessions of the monastery of Bangor*   *See ¶ 13
was not grateful for that benefice. From that time on
he was very haughty towards him and his disciples,
troublesome over everything, hatching plots everywhere and disparaging his deeds. But he did not do so
without punishment. He had but one son, who,
following his father's example, dared to act against
Malachy and died that same year. This is how he
died: Malachy thought that a stone oratory should be
built at Bangor similar to those which he had seen
erected in other places. And when he began to lay the
foundations the natives were all amazed, because no
buildings of that kind were found in the region.
That good-for-nothing was not amazed, however but
highly indignant. From that indignation he conceived
sorrow and brought forth iniquity.* He became a   *Ps 7:14
whisperer among the people,† now disparaging   †Lv 19:16
[Malachy] in private,* now openly blaspheming   *Ps 101:5
[him], pointing to the foolishness, being horrified at
the novelty, greatly bemoaning the expense. He was
urging and leading many to put a stop to the whole
thing with poisonous words of this nature. 'Follow
me,' he said. 'Let us not allow something to be done
without our permission which we ourselves should be
doing.' Then along with many whom he was able to
persuade he went down to the place and accosted the
man of God. He was the chief leader in speaking* as   *Ac 14:11
he was the initiator of the evil.

'My good man, what are you thinking of in bringing such a novelty into our area? We are Irishmen,
not Frenchmen.[169] What kind of silliness is this?

What need was there for a work so extravagant, so
haughty? How will a poor and needy man* of your
like ever get the wherewithal to finish it?† Who
will ever see it finished? What kind of presumption is
this, to begin what you can never—I do not say,
finish—but see finished. Although it is really more
the doing of a madman than mere presumption to
attempt something which surpasses all moderation,
exceeds his strength and transcends his abilities. Stop
at once, cease from this insanity. Otherwise, we do
not allow it, we do not support it.'

This he said, reporting what he wanted, not considering what he could do. For some of those he had
counted on and brought along with him, upon seeing
the man [Malachy], changed their minds and no
longer went along with him.*

¶62. To him the holy man said with complete freedom:

'You wretch! The work which you behold and
begrudge as begun will without any doubt be finished
and many shall see it finished. But you, because you
do not want it, will not see it; another thing you do
not want, you shall die. Look after yourself lest you
die in your sins.'*

And so it was. He died and the work was finished.
But he did not see it for, as we said above, he died
that same year. In the meanwhile the father, having
soon heard what the saint had predicted about his
son, knowing that his word was living and effectual,*
said, 'He has killed my son'.† And with the devil
urging him on, he was so consumed with rage against
[Malachy] that he was not afraid to accuse him
before the duke and noblemen of Ulidia of falsity
and lying. This of someone who was utterly truthful
and a disciple and lover of truth. He reviled him, calling him an ape![170] And indeed Malachy, taught not
to render railing for railing,* was silent and did not
open his mouth* while the sinner was making a case
against him:† But the Lord forgot not His word,
which He had said: Revenge is mine, I will repay.*

The same day the man returned home and he paid

*cf. Ps 37:16,
72:12
†Lk 14:28

*Jn 6:66

*Jn 8:21

*Heb 4:12
†1 K 17:18

*1 P 3:9
*Ps 39:9
†Ps 39:1-2
*Rm 12:19

for the rashness of his unbridled tongue. He was
avenged by the very instigator who had loosened his
tongue. Having seized him, the demon cast him into
a fire, but he was soon pulled out by those present,
his body slightly burnt, but his mind gone. While he
raged Malachy was called. He came and found the
accursed fellow writhing and foaming at the mouth,
terrifying everyone with horrible cries and motions.
His whole body was violently contorted and could
scarcely be held in restraint by many men. Praying
for his enemy,* that man of every perfection was   *Mt 5:44
heard—but only in part. For immediately, while the
saint prayed, the fellow opened his eyes* and   *Jn 9:14
regained his senses. An evil spirit of the Lord† was †1 S 16:14,19:7
left with him to buffet him* so he might learn   *2 Co 12:7
not to blaspheme.†   †1 Tm 1:20

We believe that he is still alive and up to this time
he is still paying for the great sin which he committed against the saint. They do say that at certain
times he is lunatic. Finally the aforementioned
possessions reverted peaceably to the place where
they belonged since he was not able to hold onto
them because of his weakness and his uselessness.
Nor did Malachy refuse them once peace had finally
been won after so much trouble.

¶63. But now our account reverts to the work of
the building which Malachy had undertaken. Malachy
did not have the funds—I won't say, to finish it—but
to do any of it. But his heart trusted in the Lord.* As   *Dn 13:35
a matter of fact, the Lord provided that, although he
put not his trust in money hordes,* money would not   *Si 31:8
be lacking. For what other person brought it about
that treasure should have been hoarded there and
being hidden away would not be found until Malachy's time and need? God's servant found in God's
purse what was lacking in his own. It was only right.
For what could be more just than for someone who,
for God's sake, had nothing of his own, since he who
had entered into fellowship with God, should have
one purse for both?* For the man who believes,   *Pr 1:14
the whole world is full of riches. And what is it if not

a sort of God's purse? In fact He says: the earth is

mine, and the fulness thereof.† So it is that Malachy
did not rebury the many silver coins he found, but
took them out to use. He ordered that God's entire
gift be expended in God's work. He took no thought
for his own needs or those of his disciples, but he cast

his thought on the Lord,* for he never hesitated to
resort to Him as often as need required. Nor is there
any doubt that this was God's work, that Malachy
had foreseen it by God's revelation. He conferred
first of all with his brethren about that work and
many gave their consent with extreme reluctance
because of the lack of means. Hence he was anxious
and doubtful what he ought to do, but he began to
make inquiry earnestly in prayer as to whatever
God's will should be. And returning from a journey
one day as he approached the place he looked at it
from some distance away. And behold a great
oratory appeared built of stone and extremely
beautiful. He considered it carefully, its position, its
shape and its arrangement, and when he undertook
the work confidently, he first told of the vision
to the older brethren, but only to a few. Certainly he
had attentively noted everything regarding the place,
manner, and quality with such diligent observation
that once the work was finished, the completed oratory was so like the one he had seen that anyone
would believe that he, with Moses, had heard it
said: 'See that you make all things according to the

pattern which was shown you on the mount'.* By
the same kind of vision the oratory, and in fact the

whole monastery built in Saul,* had been shown to
him before it was erected.

WHAT HE DID AND PREDICTED IN THE
SPIRIT OF ELIAS AND ABOUT THE
DEACON COMING TO THE ALTAR
UNWORTHILY, ABOUT THE DOVE AT
MASS; WHAT HE HAD SEEN OF THE
TOMBS OF THE SAINTS ALL ABLAZE

¶XXIX.64. As he was going through a certain city
and a great multitude[171] was gathering around him,
he happened to see among the others a young man
eager to see him. He had climbed on a stone and,
on the very tips of his toes, with his neck stretched
out, straining towards him with eyes and mind, he
appeared to be another Zacchaeus.* Nor did it   *Lk 19:4
escape Malachy's notice, the Holy Spirit revealing it
to him, that he had really come in the spirit and
power* of Zacchaeus. He pretended not to notice at   *Lk 1:17
the time and quietly passed by. But in the hospice
that night he told the brethren how he had seen him
and what he had foreseen about him. On the third
day, didn't he come with a certain nobleman, his
lord,[172] who disclosed the vow and desire of the
young man and asked that [Malachy] deign receive
the boy on his recommendation and to have him
henceforth among his own brethren. And recognizing
him, Malachy said: 'It is not necessary that men
should recommend him whom God has already
commended.'† He took him by the hand and   †2 Co 10:18
entrusted him to our Abbot Congan* and he in turn   *See Preface 2,
to the brethren. Now that young man, still alive, I   fn. 3.
assume, was the first lay brother[173] of the monastery
of the Suir.[174] According to everyone's report he
leads a holy life among the brothers according to the
Cistercian Order. And the disciples of Malachy
realized* that even in this he had the gift of   *Jn 21:4
prophecy†, and not only in this instance, but also   †Rv 19:10

in the one that we intend to add.

¶65. While he was offering the sacraments and the deacon approached him to do something proper to his ministry, the priest looked steadily at him. And he groaned because he had felt that something improper lay hidden in him. When, after the sacrifice had been completed, he was questioned secretly about his conscience, he confessed and denied not* that he had suffered pollution[175] in a dream that night. Malachy imposed a penance upon him saying: 'You should not have ministered today, but to have withdrawn yourself modestly from holy things, and to have shown deference to such great divine mysteries, so that purged by this humility, you might hereafter exercise your ministry more worthily.'

*Jn 1:20

At another time he was offering the sacrifice and praying at the time of the Sacrifice with that holiness and purity of heart which was his usual attitude. As the deacon stood near him, a dove appeared, entering the window in great brilliance. The priest was entirely bathed in it and the entire gloomy church shone with it. The dove flew about for awhile, finally perching on the cross in front of the priest. The deacon was amazed, fearful partly because of the unusual brightness and partly because of the unusual bird, for it is a rare bird in that land. He fell on his face* trembling and hardly dared to rise even when the duties of his ministry required it. After Mass Malachy took him aside and cautioned him, at the peril of his life never to let slip* the secret he had witnessed as long as he lived.

*Ezk 43:3

*Mt 17:9, Mk 9:9, Lk 9:36

Once while he was at Armagh with one of his auxiliary bishops he arose early* and, praying, began to make the rounds of the saints' tombs, of which there are many in the cemetery of Saint Patrick.[176] And lo, they saw one of the altars suddenly catch fire. Both of them saw this great vision and both were astonished. Now Malachy, sensing that this was a sign of the great merit of him[177] or of those who rested beneath the altar, ran and plunged himself into the midst of the flames, embracing the holy

*Jr 25:3, 26:5

altar with outstretched arms. What he did or what he
felt there, no one knows except this: he came out of
that fire more ablaze than usual with a heavenly fire.
I think that none of the brethren who were with him
do not know.

THE TRULY APOSTOLIC MAN EMBEL-
LISHED WITH MANY MIRACLES OF
EVERY KIND (ALTHOUGH FEW ARE MEN-
TIONED HERE) WHILE ON A JOURNEY
BACK TO ROME FELL ASLEEP IN THE
LORD AT ·CLAIRVAUX ON THE DAY
WHICH HE HAD HOPED FOR AND FORE-
TOLD, YET HE EVER LIVES TO MAKE
Heb 7:25   INTERCESSION FOR US*

¶66. These things have been said, a few indeed out
of many, but enough for our time. For these are not
the times for signs according to that saying: Our
Ps 74:9   signs we have not seen; there is now no prophet.*
From this it should be sufficiently obvious how great
in his merits was my Malachy, who was so rich in
signs now very rarely to be found. For in what type
of ancient miracles[178] did Malachy not excel? If we
¶ ¶36,48,52,57,   pay earnest heed to those few which I mentioned
62, and 64.   above, he did not lack prophecy* or revelation†
† ¶ ¶11,63,64,65. or revenge upon the ungodly,§ or the grace of
§ ¶ ¶22,23,48,57,
60, and 62.   heeling,‡ or changing of minds,* or even raising of
‡1 Co 12:9; ¶ ¶   the dead.# In all these, God was blessed,* who
14,15,40,45-47,   loved him so very much and adorned him and who
49,52,61, and 62.
‡¶ ¶26,54,57,61.   made him great in the sight of kings‡ and gave him
#¶53.   the crown of glory.§ That love is proved by his
Ps 66:20.   merits, that adornment by the signs [he worked] ; his
‡Si 45:3, ¶ ¶
10,40,60.   greatness by his revenge upon his enemies, and his
§Si 47:7,   glory in the bestowal of rewards. You have, careful
1 P 5:4.   reader, something in my Malachy which you may
admire; something you may imitate. Pay close attention now to what you may expect for yourself from
Rm 6:21,   these things. For the end of these things is a
Ps 116:15   precious death.*

¶XXX.67. Once he was asked where he would

choose to spend his last day if the choice were his. It
seems that the brethren used to ask one another*
which place each would pick out for himself. He
hedged and gave no answer. When they kept insisting, he said: 'If I should depart from here[179] there is
no place I should rather die than where I could rise
with our Apostle.'[180] He was referring, of course, to
Saint Patrick. 'If I happened to be on a journey and
God so permits it, I have chosen Clairvaux.' Asked
also about the time, he replied that it should be on
All Souls' Day.[181] If this is thought of as a mere
wish, it was fulfilled; but if as a prophecy, not one
iota was lacking.* As we have heard, so have we
seen,† both as to the place and to the time. Let us
recount briefly in what order and on what occasion
this came about. He was distressed that up to this
time Ireland was without the *pallium*[182] and being
zealous for the sacraments he was naturally desirous
that his own people should not be deprived of any
of them.[183] He recalled that it had been promised to
him by Pope Innocent, hence he was the more
saddened that it had not been sent for while he was
still alive.* And realizing his opportunity now that
Pope Eugene[184] was chief pontiff and that he was
reported to be travelling to France at that very time,
he was overjoyed to have found an opportunity to
ask for the *pallium*.

He took this for granted of Eugene, being the
man he was and having been raised from religious
profession [to the Papacy] and still more because
he had been a spiritual son of his own Clairvaux; he
did not fear any difficulties as far as was concerned.
So the bishops were assembled for a council.* Three
days were spent on urgent matters and on the fourth
day they discussed obtaining the *pallium*. The motion
was passed, but only if someone else should ask for
it. But since the journey would be a short one[185]
and for that reason not too arduous, no one
opposed his plan and desire. Once he had dissolved
the council Malachy set forth on the journey.[186]
Some few of the brethren who had been present at
the council accompanied him as far as the shore.

Mk 9:33

Mt 5:18
†Ps 48:8

*¶38

*¶38

One of them, named Catholicus, called out to him
with tearful voice and countenance: 'Alas! you are
going away and you yourself know what trouble I
endure almost every day. And merciful though you
are, you are no help to me. Even if I deserve to suffer,
how have the brethren sinned that they are not
allowed to have a day or night free from caring and
looking after me?'

At these words and the tears of his son, he wept.
His fatherly feeling shaken, he embraced him, sooth-
ing him and marking on his breast the sign of the
cross. 'Rest assured,' he said, 'that you will suffer
nothing of this kind until I return.' Now the man was
an epileptic and used to fall frequently, not once but
more often every day. He had suffered with this horrible affliction for six years, but at Malachy's word he
was perfectly cured. From that hour he suffered no
such attack and we believe he will suffer none from
now on, because Malachy is never to return again.

¶68. While he was embarking, two of those who
were more dear to him came up and made bold to ask

Mt 20:20

something from him.* 'What do you want?' he
asked them. 'We will not say,' they replied, 'unless
you promise to grant it.' He promised. They went
on: 'We want you to make a firm promise on your
honor that you will return to Ireland safe and
sound.'[187] All the others insisted too. Then he pon-
dered for awhile, at first regretting that he had committed himself, but he found no way out. He was

Dn 13:22

straitened on every side,* while nothing happened on
either side to save him from the double peril—that is,
breaking either his wish or his promise. Finally it
seemed best to him to choose that which the
present moment demanded, leaving the rest to
heaven's disposition. He agreed, reluctantly, for he
did not wish to sadden them further, and he
boarded the ship, promising what they wanted. And
when they had gone about half way by sea, suddenly

Mt 14:24

a contrary wind* drove the ship back and brought it
once more to Ireland. He disembarked and spent the
night in one of his own churches in the very port.

And relieved, he gave thanks for the plan of divine providence by which it had come about that he had now fulfilled his promise. In the morning he went aboard the ship and he came into Scotland the same day with a good crossing. On the third day[188] he arrived at a place called Viride Stagnum[189] which he had prepared beforehand so that he might establish an abbey there. There he left some of his sons—our brothers—as a convent of monks with an abbot.[190] He had taken them along with him with that in mind. He wished them farewell and continued on.*   *Ac 20:1

¶69. And as he journeyed along King David[191] met him and received him with great joy. He was entertained there for several days. When he had done many things pleasing to God he continued the journey he had begun. He progressed through Scotland, making a detour to the church of Gisburn[192] at the very borders of England. Here dwell religious men[193] living the canonical life,[194] men known to him for a long time by reason of their religious life and their reputation. There a girl was brought to him suffering the disease horrible to look at—commonly they call it cancer. He cured her. When he blessed water and it was sprinkled on the ulcerated spots she felt no pain. On the following day the ulcers could scarcely be seen.

Leaving, there he came to the sea, but was refused passage. Unless I am mistaken the reason was that some misunderstanding had arisen between the Supreme Pontiff and the King of England.[195] What evil the king suspected of that good man if he should cross [the sea] I do not know. He did not permit other bishops to make the crossing either.[196] Obstacle indeed this was and contrary to Malachy's wishes but not to his intention. He grieved that his desire was postponed, little realizing how it was actually to be fulfilled. Had he crossed over right away he would have had to bypass Clairvaux in order to follow the Supreme Pontiff.[197] By that time he had already left and was at Rome or at least close to Rome. But with the delay slowing him down, Malachy made the

crossing later and so came in good season to the
place and the hour of his most holy death.[198]

¶XXXI.70. Malachy was received as the true Orient
from on high visiting us,[199] although he arrived from
the west. Oh, what great brightness did that radiant
sun add to our Clairvaux! What a joyous feast day
dawned for us at his coming! That day which the
Lord has given us, how we rejoiced and were glad in
it.* How I came running with a leap and a bound,†
shaking and weak as I was.[200] How happily I rushed
to kiss him! With what happy arms I embraced* the
grace sent me from heaven! With what eager face and
mind, my Father, I brought you into my mother's
house, and into the chamber of her who bore me.*
What festive days I spent with you then, but all too
few! In his turn, how did he fare with us? Our pilgrim
bore himself truly joyous, truly affable to all,
unbelievably thankful to all. How good and how
pleasant* a guest who was among us, whom he had
come from the ends of the earth to see, not to hear,
but to show himself a Salomon. Then we heard his
wisdom,* we held him present and we still hold him.

Some four or five days of this festival of ours had
gone by, when suddenly he came down with a fever
and took to his bed. And all of us were sick along
with him.[201] The end of our mirth is sadness,* more
moderate perhaps, because the fever seemed light for
a time. You could see the brethren running about
eager to give or to receive. To whom was it not sweet
to behold him? To whom was it not sweeter to
minister to him? Both were sweet and both were
salutary. To do him a service as human kindness and
once offered it brought grace back to each one. Everyone was at hand; everyone was there, solicitous with
much serving,* seeking medicine, applying poltices,
more often urging him to eat. To them he said:
'These things are to no avail, but I shall do what you
command me because I love you.' For he knew that
the time of his departure was close at hand.

¶71. When the brethren who had come with him

*Ps 118:24
†celer et saliens

*Gn 29:13

*Sg 3:4

*Ps 133:1

*Mt 12:42

*Pr 14:13

*Lk 10:40

kept more boldly, saying that he ought not to despair of life—there were no signs of death apparent in him[202] he replied: 'It is fitting that Malachy go forth from his body this year.' And he added:

'Look, the day is approaching which, as you know full well, I have always hoped would be the day of my release.* I know whom I have believed and I am certain† that I shall not be cheated of the rest of my desire,* I already have part of it. He who has brought me to the place I asked for, will by the same token not deny me the end I desired. So far as my poor body is concerned, here is my rest.* As for my soul, the Lord will provide,* who saves those who trust in him.* Nor is there small hope laid up for me on that day* on which so much great good favor is expended by the living for the dead.'[203]

*2 Tm 4:6
†2 Tm 1:12
*Ps 78:30

*Ps 132:14,
Is 28:12
*Gn 22:8
*Ps 17:6
*2 Tm 4:8

Nor was that day very far off when he said these things. In the meantime he orders that he be anointed with holy oil. As the community of the brethren began processing to perform this solemnly,[204] he would not allow them to come up to him, but he went down to them. He was lying in a loft[205] in the upper house. He was anointed and after receiving the *Viaticum* and commending himself to the brethren's prayers, and the brethren to God,[206] he returned to his bed. He had come down from the high loft on his own feet and he went upstairs again no less on his feet, and he kept saying death was at the door.* Who would believe that this man was on the point of death? Only he alone and God could have known it. His face did not appear paler or leaner,[207] his brow was not wrinkled, his eyes not sunken, his nostrils not pinched, his lips not drawn, his teeth not blackened, his neck not gaunt and scrawny, his shoulders not curved, the flesh on the rest of his body was not dried up. This was his bodily grace and this the glory of his countenance which does not become vacant,* not even in death. As he was as long as he lived, so he was in death, more like a living man.

*Mt 24:33

*2 Co 3:7

¶72. We have been running up to now, but here we hold fast because Malachy has finished his course.*

*1 Tm 4:7

He is still and we with him are likewise still. Besides, who would willingly run towards death? Especially your death, holy father, who could report it? Who would want to listen? Yet we loved each other in life, in death we shall not be parted.* Brothers, let us not forsake in death the one whom we accompanied in life. From Further Scotland* he ran here to his death. Let us go too and die with him.† It is appropriate, very appropriate, to say what it was necessary to perceive. The Feast of All Saints, everywhere a high feast, is now, but according to the old saying: 'A tale out of time is like music in mourning.'* We are here present; we sing, but unwillingly. We sing in our weeping and we weep in our singing. Malachy, though he does not sing, does not weep either. Why would he mourn, he is approaching joy? For us who are left,* mourning is left; only Malachy keeps the feast. For what he cannot do with his body he performs with his mind as was written: The thought of man shall give you praise, and the remainders of thought shall keep holiday for you.* Since the instrument of his body has failed him, and the organ of the mouth is mute, and the service of the voice stops, it remains that he should keep the feast with jubilation of the mind. Why should he not keep the feast with the saints, he is being taken to the festival of the saints?[208] He shows them what is soon to be owed to himself. Yet a little while* and he is one of them.

¶73. Along about dusk when we had finished the day's celebration, Malachy was approaching not dusk but dawn. For is it not dawn for someone for whom the night has passed and the day is at hand?* Then as the fever increased a burning sweat from within began to appear all over his body, so that somehow passing through fire and water he might be brought into a refreshing place.* Now we despaired of his life, now everyone found fault with his own judgment; now there was no doubt in anyone's mind that Malachy's prediction would prevail.* We are called. We came. And raising his eyes to the bystanders he said: 'With

*2 S 1:23

*Ab ulteriori
  Scotia=*Ireland*

†Jn 11:16

*Si 22:6

*1 Th 4:16

*Ps 76:11

*Jn 7:33

*Rm 13:12

*Ps 66:12

*¶71

desire I have desired to eat this Passover with you.*   *Lk 22:15*
I am thankful for heaven's compassion. I am not
cheated of my desire.'* Do you behold the man   *Ps 78:30*
composed in death and not yet dead, now certain of
life? No wonder. Seeing that the night he had looked
forward to was at hand and that in it his day was
dawning, as it were triumphing over night, he seemed
to deride the darkness and to speak out: 'Now I will
not say:* "Perhaps darkness shall cover me, and night   *Jn 15:15*
shall be my light in my pleasure." '* And comforting   *Ps 139:11*
us gently, he said: 'Have a care for me; if at all
possible I shall not forget you. And it shall be
allowed. I have believed in God and all things are
possible to him who believes.* I have loved God, I   *Mk 9:22*
have loved you; and charity never passes away.'†   †1 Co 13:8
And looking up to heaven,* he said: 'Oh God!   *Mk 7:34*
Keep them in your name;† not only them, but all   †Jn 17:11
those, too, who through my .word* and ministry   *Jn 17:20*
have given themselves to your service.' Then, laying
his hands upon each one of them* and blessing them   *Mk 10:16*
all,† he bade them get some rest, because his hour   †Lk 4:40
had not yet come.*   *Jn 2:4*

¶74. We left and returned about midnight for it is
said that light shines in the darkness* at that hour.   *Jn 1:5*
The house was full, the entire community was at
hand, including many abbots who had gathered
together. With psalms, hymns and spiritual canticles*   *Eph 5:19,
we follow our friend as he goes home.²⁰⁹ In the   Col 3:16
fifty-fourth year of his age, at the place and at the
time he had forechosen and foretold²¹⁰ Malachy,
bishop and legate of the holy Apostolic See, fell   *Ac 7:60
asleep happily in the Lord,* taken by angels† from   †Lk 16:22
our hands. And he really did fall asleep; his peaceful
face was the sign of a peaceful death. Everyone's eyes
were fixed on him,* but no one was able to perceive   *Lk 4:20
when he departed. When dead he was thought to be
living; when alive he was thought dead. Nothing
really happened to mark the dividing line between
them. That liveliness of countenance, that peaceful-
ness such as is apparent in a sleeper—you could say
that death took away none of these, but rather it
increased them greatly. He was not changed, but he

changed all of us. In a wonderful way everyone's
sorrow and sighing suddenly ceased; sadness was
turned into joy,* singing banished mourning.

He is carried out, voices are raised to heaven, he is
carried into the oratory on the shoulders of the
abbots. Faith has been victorious,* love conquers;
things fall back into routine. Everything is orderly
done, everything proceeds reasonably.

¶75. And truth to tell, what reason should there be
to mourn for Malachy immoderately, as though his
death were not precious,* as though it were not
rather sleep than death, as though it were not the
port of death and the portal to life. Our friend Malachy is asleep* and do I mourn? Such grief is main-
tained by custom, not by reason. If the Lord has
given sleep to his beloved and such sleep in which the
inheritance of the Lord are children, the reward the
fruit of the womb,* which of these would seem to
call for tears? Shall I weep for him who is beyond
all weeping? He is dancing, he is triumphing, he has
been led into the joy of the Lord*—and I should
mourn for him? I desire these things for myself; I do
not envy him. In the meanwhile the funeral rites are
made ready, the Sacrifice is offered for him,[211]
everything is carried out according to custom with
the greatest devotion.

There was a lad standing off at a distance and his
arm hung lifeless at his side, more of a nuisance to the
boy than useful. When I noticed him I made a sign
for him to approach. I took the withered hand and
laid it on the bishop's hand and he brought it back to
life.* Surely the grace of healing† lived in the dead
man; his hand was to the lifeless hand what Elisha was
to the lifeless man.* The lad had come from a long
way off† and the hand which he had brought hang-
ing down lifeless he took back to his country cured.

Now when everything had been done according to
ritual in the very oratory in which he was well
pleased.[212] Malachy was committed to his grave, on
the fourth of the Nones of November in the eleven
hundred and forty-eighth year of the Incarnation of

*Est 13:17, 16:21,
Jm 4:9

*1 Jn 5:4

*Ps 116:15

*Jn 11:11

*Ps 127:2-3

*Mt 25:21, 23

*Mt 12:10
†1 Co 12:9

*2 K 4:18 ff.
†Mk 8:3

the Lord. Good Jesus! yours is the deposit[213] which
was entrusted to us.* Yours is the treasure which is   **1 Tm 1:11*
buried with us. We are keeping it to be transferred to
you at the time when you propose to demand it.
Only grant that he may not go forth without his own
        comrades,[214] but may we have him as our
          leader whom we had as our guest and
           grant we may reign with you
             and   with   him   too,
               for ever and ever.*   **Rv 22:5*
                Amen.

Bernard of Clairvaux

SERMON ON THE PASSING
OF SAINT MALACHY
THE BISHOP

SERMON ON THE PASSING
OF SAINT MALACHY
THE BISHOP

M Y MOST DEARLY beloved, an abundant blessing has descended on you from heaven this day. You should suffer loss, yet I would be in danger, had I not faithfully apportioned it, for it seems to me this duty has been entrusted to me. Still I fear for your loss and my damnation, in case it be said: 'The young children ask for bread and no one offers it to them.'*[215] I *Lm 4:4* know how necessary for you is the consolation coming down from heaven, since it is certain that you have manfully sworn off all carnal pleasures and earthly allurements. No one could entertain a doubt that it was all a gift from heaven and in the divine plan* that Bishop Malachy should fall asleep among *cf. Ac 2:23* you today and to be buried here as he had desired.* *Life ¶67* When not a single leaf of a tree falls to the ground without God's will,* is anyone so stupid that he does *Mt 10:29* not plainly see in the coming and the passing of this truly great plan of divine goodness? He came from the ends of the earth to be buried here in our earth. He was bent upon another errand, to be sure, but because of his special love for us, we know it was that which he desired most of all. Certainly he experienced many delays on the journey itself, having been denied permission to sail until the time of his end was drawing near and the goal which could not be reached.[216] We received him who had come to us by many hardships as an angel sent from God,* out *Ga 4:14* of reverence for his holiness. And he received us out of his deeply engrained humility and gentleness* *Eph 4:2*

97

with love far greater than we deserved. Then he spent
but a few days with us in good health, awaiting his
brethren who were still scattered about England
because the ill-founded suspicions of the king
thwarted the man of God. But when they had all
come together and he was preparing for the journey
to Rome for which he had come, he was overtaken
suddenly by sickness and he sensed at once that he
was being called instead to the heavenly court. God
foresaw something better for us, lest Malachy in

Heb 11:40   going away from us should be perfected elsewhere.

¶2. To the physicians there appeared no sign of
serious illness, much less of death. Yet he, in merry
spirits, said that it was completely befitting that
Life ¶71   Malachy should this year pass from this life. Great
pains were taken against this both in fervent prayers
to God and in every way we could, but his merits so
won the day that his heart's desire was granted him
Ps 21:2   and the request of his lips was not withdrawn. So it
was that everything happened to concur with his own
wishes: that he had chosen for himself this of all
places by divine inspiration and that he had long
desired as the day of his burial that day on which the
general commemoration of all the faithful is cele-
Life ¶¶67,71 brated. But this has also quite rightly increased our
joy: that the same day had been chosen, by God's
instigation, for the re-burial of our brethren's bones
which had been brought from the earlier cemetery.[217]
As we were bringing in the remains and singing the
customary psalms, the holy man kept saying how
greatly this chant delighted him. And not long after-
ward he himself followed, sunk into a blissful and
refreshing sleep. We give thanks therefore to God for
all his dispositions: that he deigned to honor us
though unworthy with the presence of Malachy's
holy death; that he enriched his poor men with the
very precious treasure of his body, that he chose to
support us who are weak by so great a pillar of his
Ga 2:9   Church. Because one or another of two signs proves
†Ps 86:17   a thing was done for our good,† either that this
place is pleasing to God or that he wishes to render

it pleasing to himself, he led this man of outstanding
holiness from the ends of the earth* here to die and   *Mt 12:42
here to be buried.

¶3. Our very love for this holy father compels us to
grieve more deeply along with that people and to
shudder more violently at the cruelty of death which
has not refrained from afflicting the Church with so
terrible a wound. Death surely is awful and inexor-
able. It has penalized a great crowd of men by striking
down this one of them. Blind and improvident, it has
tied Malachy's tongue, shackled his footsteps, relaxed
his hands, and closed his eyes. Those faithful eyes,
I say, which by their tender, loving tears used to
bring divine grace to sinners. Those undefiled hands
which had always loved to be exercised in laborious
and humble deeds, which had so often offered up for
sinners the saving host* of the Lord's body and were   *2 M 3:32
lifted up to heaven in prayer without anger or con-
tention;* which are known to have conferred many   *1 Tm 2:8
blessings on the sick and to have shone with various
signs. The beautiful footsteps of him who preached
the gospel of peace and brought glad tidings of good
things.* The feet so often wearied in the eagerness of   *Rm 10:15,
loving mercy. Those footsteps always worthy to be   Is 52:7
pressed with devout kisses.²¹⁸ Finally those holy lips
of the priest which guarded knowledge;* the mouth   *Ml 2:7
of the just which shall meditate wisdom and his
tongue which shall speak judgment,* yes, and mercy   *Ps 37:30
too.* By ·these he used to cure great wounds of souls.   *Ps 101:1
Nor should we wonder, brothers, that death is full of
iniquity when iniquity itself brought forth death,*   *Jm 1:15
that it is a thoughtless thing, born as it was of
seduction.* Nor should we marvel, I repeat, if it   *2 Co 11:3
strikes without discernment, when it came from a
transgression;* if it is cruel and heedless when it has   *1 Tm 2:14
come forth from the trickery of the old serpent*   *Rv 12:9, 20:2
and from the folly of the woman. But why do we
dispute that it dared to assail Malachy, a faithful
member of Christ,* when it attacked as well Mala-   *1 Co 6:15
chy's head, and the head of all the chosen people as
well? It rushed upon the guiltless who was not to

Eph 4:15

1 Co 15:59, 2 Co 5:4

suffer, but it did not escape guiltless.* Death struck against life, but life came to grips with death and was swallowed up in life.* It gobbled up the hook for itself. Thereafter it began to be held by Him whom it seemed to have held.[219]

¶4. But perhaps someone may say: 'How does death seem to be overcome by the head, if it still rages in freedom against the members? If death is dead,[220] how did it kill Malachy? If conquered, how does it still prevail over everyone, and there is no man that

Ps 89:48
1 Jn 3:8

shall live and not see death?'* Clearly death has been conquered—the work of the devil* and the penalty of sin. Sin—the cause of death—has likewise been conquered. The wicked one—himself the author of sin

1 Jn 2:13, 14

and death—is conquered.* Not only are they conquered; they have already been judged and condemned. Their sentence is divided certainly, but not yet publicly proclaimed. The fire is already prepared

Mt 25:41

for the devil,* even though he is not yet cast into it. He is still allowed to continue his evil practices for a

Rv 12:12

short while longer.* He has been made the hammer of the Heavenly Artificer, the hammer of the whole

Jr 50:23
†*1 Co 12:7*

earth.* He wears down the elect for their own profit;† he pulverizes the evil one for their con-demnation. As the master of the household is, so are

Mt 10:25

those of his household,* which means sin and death. It is not to be doubted that although sin was

Col 2:14

nailed to the cross with Christ,* still it was allowed while not to rule yet to reside for a time in the Apostle while he lived. Call me a liar if he does not himself say: Now it is no more I that do it, but sin

Rm 7:17

that dwells in me.* So too death itself is not yet compelled to get away, but it is forced not to get in the way. However, there will be a time when it will

1 Co 15:55
1 Co 15:26

be said: O death, where is your victory?* Death is surely the last enemy that shall be destroyed.* Now indeed since He rules who has the power of life

Ws 16:13

and death* and even confines the sea within the fixed boundaries of its shores, death itself is to the Lord's beloved but a refreshing sleep. To this the prophet witnesses who says: For he shall give sleep

to his beloved, behold the inheritance of the Lord.*   *Ps 127:2-3
The death of the wicked is very evil,† for their birth   †Ps 34:21
is evil and their life is worse. But precious is the
death of the saints.* Clearly it is precious, for it is the   *Ps 116:15
end of their labors, the consummation of victory as
it were, the gate of life and the entrance to perfect
security.

¶5. Therefore, brothers, let us be glad, let us rejoice (as is fitting) with our father, for it is an act of
devotion to mourn Malachy dead and a much greater
devotion to rejoice with him alive. Isn't he alive?
Happily alive! To the eyes of the foolish he seemed
to be dead,[221] of course, but he is at peace, now at
last a fellow-citizen of the saints and a member of the
household of God.* He sings with them and he gives   *Eph 2:19
thanks saying: We have passed through fire and
water, and you have brought us out into a place of
refreshment.* He passed through manfully, it is   *Ps 66:12
evident, and he went through happily. The true
Hebrew celebrated Passover in spirit and going along
he said to us: With desire I have desired to eat this
Passover with you.* He passed through fire and   *Lk 22:15
water,† he whom sadness could not break nor ease   †Ps 66:12
detain. There is below us a place which fire claims so
entirely as its own that the miserable rich man there
could not have even a single drop of water from the
finger of Lazarus.* And there is above the City of   *Lk 16:24-25
God, which the streams of the river make glad,* a   *Ps 46:4
torrent of pleasure,† a cup which inebriates so   †Ps 36:8
richly.* Here in its very midst is contained the   *Ps 23:5
knowledge of good and evil* and here one under-   *Gn 2:9
goes the trial of pleasure and tribulation.* Eve the   *2 Co 8:2
unfortunate brought us into these vicissitudes. Here,
of course, there is day and night, but in hell there is
only night and in heaven only day.* Happy the soul   *Rv 21:25, 22:5
therefore who passes through both, neither suc-
cumbing to pleasure nor fainting at tribulation.*   *Eph 3:13

¶6. I think I should tell you briefly about some of
the many fine miracles of this man by which we
recognize that he did pass very bravely through fire

*Ps 66:12

*Life ¶ ¶19 ff.
*cf. Ps 83:12

*1 S 19:5,
 Ps 119:109

*Life ¶ ¶19-31

*Ps 17:3, 66:10-11

and water.* A tyrannical race claimed the metropolitan see of Patrick, the great apostle of the Irish, creating archbishops in regular succession,* possessing the sanctuary of God by heredity*. Our beloved Malachy, begged by the faithful to stand up to such great evils, took his life in his hands* and went forward bravely. He took on the bishopric, putting himself in great danger so that he might put an end to so great an injustice. He ruled the Church amidst perils, but once the perils were gone he immediately ordained someone else to succeed him in true canonical fashion. For it was on this stipulation that he had accepted the office: that later on, once the fury of persecution had passed, he would be able to appoint someone else. He wanted to be allowed to go back once again to his own see,* where he lived in the religious community which he had himself founded, without ecclesiastical or worldly benefices. Until now he has lived among them as one of them without any goods of his own. Thus the fire of tribulation* tried the man of God, but it did not consume him.[222] Surely he was gold. Likewise pleasure did not tempt and destroy him nor did he stand still as an idle spectator on the road, heedless of his own pilgrimage.

¶7. Which one of you, brothers, would not passionately desire to imitate his holiness, should one even dare to hope for it? I believe that you will listen more eagerly if I tell you what made Malachy holy. But should my testimony seem less than acceptable, listen to what Scripture has to say: He made him holy in faith and meekness.* By faith he trampled underfoot the world, as John witnesses who said: This is the victory which overcomes the world, our faith.* For in the spirit of meekness† he endured with good cheer‡ everything that was hard and contrary. Like Christ he trampled upon the seas* so that he would not be snared by enticements and he possessed his soul in patience† so that he would not be crushed by troubles. Of both these things you have examples in the Psalms: A thousand shall fall by

*Si 45:4

*1 Jn 5:4
†Ga 6:1
‡1 K 21:7
*Mt 14:25,
 Jn 6:19

†Lk 21:19

your side and ten thousand at your right hand.* For   *Ps 91:7
how many more fall to the false promises of prosperity than to the scourge of adversity? Dear brothers,
let no one of us then be deceived by the level surface
of an easier way into imagining that the path of the
sea would be more comfortable for us. Here the
plain holds great mountains, imperceptible to be
sure, but more dangerous for that very reason. The
was passing through steep hills and rugged rocks
may seem far more laborious, but to the experienced
it is found to be far safer and more desirable. On
both paths there is struggle, on both there is danger
everywhere, as he well knew who said: by the armor
of justice on the right hand and on the left.* Thus we   *2 Co 6:7
may rejoice with those who have passed through fire
and water and have come into a place of refreshment.* Do you want to hear about this place of   *Ps 66:12
refreshment? If only someone else would tell you
about it! Myself, I cannot spew forth what I have
never tasted.

¶8. Today I seem to hear Malachy speaking to me
about that place of refreshment: Turn, O my soul, to
your rest; for the Lord has been generous to you, for
he has delivered my soul from death—and so on.*   *Ps 114:7-8
Listen to what few words I have to say, for the day is
far spent,* and this sermon has gone on longer than   *Lk 24:29
I had hoped because I am unwillingly torn away from
the sweet name of our father and my tongue flinches
to cease speaking of Malachy. My brothers, the death
of the soul* is sin, unless perhaps what you read in   *Ps 115:8
the Prophet has escaped you: The soul that sins, the
same shall die.* Threefold then is the rejoicing of   *Ezk 18:4
the man who has been freed from all sin and labor
and danger. From now on neither is sin said to dwell
in him* nor is the sorrow of penitence declared   *Rm 7:17, 20
nor from then on is he warned to guard himself
against any fall. Elijah has put down his *pallium*.* It   *2 K 2:8
was not what he feared: it was not that he feared it
might be touched or even taken by an adulteress.*   *Gn 39:12, 15
He climbs into the chariot.† Now he is not afraid he   *2 K 2:11
may fall. He mounts up joyfully, not laboring to fly

*Sg 1:3

*Sg 1:3-4

under his own power, but sitting in a swift chariot. Let us, beloved, run to this place of refreshment, eager in spirit, in the odor of the ointments* of our blessed father who we see this day to have stirred up our sluggish spirits to a burning, ardent desire. Let us run after him, I say, crying out continuously: 'Draw us after you.'* In the affection of our hearts and the perfection of our conversion, let us return, devout thanks to Almighty and merciful [God] that He has willed that we, unworthy servants utterly without merits of our own, are at least never without someone else's prayers.

Bernard of Clairvaux

HOMILY ON THE
ANNIVERSARY OF THE DEATH
OF SAINT MALACHY

HOMILY ON THE
ANNIVERSARY OF THE DEATH
OF SAINT MALACHY[223]

I T IS ALL TOO CLEAR, most dearly beloved, that while we are in the body we wander[224] absent from the Lord.* Our exile[224] here and the realization of our own faults certainly commits us rather to sorrow than to joy. But we are admonished by the words of the Apostle to rejoice with them that rejoice;* the time and the occasion require that we be roused up to all gladness. For if it is true, as the Prophet observed, that the just rejoice in God's sight,* then Malachy is doubtless rejoicing, who in his days pleased God and was found just.* He ministered in holiness and justice before Him,† to Him both minister and ministry were pleasing. And why should he not have pleased Him? He delivered the Gospel without charge.* He filled the country with the Gospel. He tamed the deadly barbarism of the Irish. With the sword of the Spirit,* he conquered foreign peoples to the light yoke of Christ,* restoring his inheritance to Him† even to the ends of the earth.* O fruitful minister! Is not the Father's promise to the Son fulfilled through him? Did not the Father look to him long ago when he said to the Son: 'I will give you the peoples for your inheritance and the ends of the earth for your possessions'?* How willingly the Saviour received what he had bought,† and had bought with the price of his own blood* by the ignominy of the Cross, by the terror of the Passion! How willingly from Malachy's hands, because he ministered freely!* Therefore there was in the minister a pleasing sight freely

*2 Co 5:6

*Rm 12:15

*Ps 68:3
*Si 50:1 & 44:
16-17. The Anti-
phon for Lauds
of a bishop
confessor.
†Lk 1:75

*1 Co 9:18.
Life ¶43

*Mt 11:30

*Eph 6:17, Ws 8:14
†Ps 16:5
*Is 48:20,
Jer 25:31

*Ps 2:8
†2 P 2:1
*1 Co 6:20,
1 P 1:18-19

*1 Co 11:7

*gratum erat
munus gratuitum

*Mt 6:22,
Lk 11:34
*Heb 3:13

offered,* and in his ministry the pleasing conversion
of sinners. Gracious, I say, and pleasing in the minister
was the simplicity of his eye,* in his ministry the salvation of the people.*

¶2. Yet although a less effective ministry would
follow, nevertheless He quite rightly respected Malachy and his works. Purity is His friend and simplicity
a member of His household and His is the right to
weigh the intentions of a task, to estimate from the
appearance of the eye the condition of the whole

*Mt 6:22-23,
Lk 11:34-35
*Ps 111:2
†Gn 1:31

body.* Now truly, great are the works of the Lord,
sought out in all the desires* and efforts of Malachy.
They are great and many and exceedingly good,†
but even better because of the good origin of a pure
intention. What work of piety escaped Malachy's
notice? Himself poor, he was rich to the poor. He

*Ps 68:5

*2 Co 9:7

was father to orphans,* husband to widows, protector of the oppressed. Cheerfully he gave,* seldom
begged a boon, modestly accepted them. He was
particularly anxious about and very successful in
restoring peace to those in disagreement. Who was as
sympathetic as he was in sharing the sorrows of
others, or so prompt in offering help, or so free in
upbraiding? For he was full of zeal, but he knew how

*1 Co 9:22

to keep it in bounds. With the weak he was weak,*
yet nevertheless powerful among the strong. He

*Jm 4:6,
1 P 5:5

resisted the proud,* he lashed out at tyrants, himself
a teacher of kings and of princes. He it was who by
prayer took the sight from a king working harm, but

*Life ¶60

restored it to him once humbled.* He it was who
forced to peace those men who had broken the
peace, who had given themselves up to the spirit of

*1 Jn 4:6

error.* He tricked them in the very evil they had
plotted against him and they were surely confounded
and astounded at what happened to them. He it was
for whom a river most obliging flowed against those

*Jos 7:15

who had likewise violated a pact.* Marvellously
putting itself before them, it voided the undertakings

*Life ¶ ¶58-59

of the ungodly.* There had been no storms, no
flood of waters, no gathering of clouds, no melting of
snows, when suddenly what had been a rivulet

became a mighty river. It went rushing along and swelled into a flood and utterly blocked the passage of those who wished to do evil.

¶3. What great things we have heard and known* of the zeal of the man and the vengeance of his enemies when he was sweet and mild and plenteous in mercy to all* who suffered need. He lived as though he were the one father of all.[225] He cuddled them all and he protected them under the shelter of his wings,† as a hen gathers her chickens.* He did not distinguish sex, age, condition or person;† he left no one out, embracing everyone in his merciful heart. No matter what the affliction of which someone complained to him, he considered it his own, but even more, patient in his own tribulation, he was sympathetic and, I may add, overly passionate in regard to others.[226] Indeed he was not infrequently filled with wrath, deeply stirred to take the part of one against another, that by delivering the weak and restraining the strong* he should thereby consider the salvation of all. So he used to get angry, but it was lest he should sin by not being angry, according to that word from the Psalm: Be angry and sin not.* Anger did not rule him, but he himself ruled his spirit.* He had control over himself. Being victor over himself he could not be overcome by anger.* He kept his anger in hand; when it was evoked it came forth, but did not erupt. It was brought forth by consent, it by blind impulse, and he was not set on fire by it, but used it.[227] Both his accuracy of judgment and his caution were great in this matter, as in ruling and controlling all the impulses of the exterior and interior man.* He did not pay so much attention to others that he left himself alone out of consideration so as to disregard himself in caring for all the rest. He was careful of himself, guarding himself well. In a word, he was so entirely his own and so entirely everyone's that it would seem his charity could not keep him or impede him in any way from care for himself, nor his concern for himself from the good of all.* If you were to see the man involved in the midst

*Ps 78:3

*Ps 86:5

†Ps 61:4
*Mt 23:37
*Life ¶42

*Ps 35:10

*Ps 4:5
*Prov 16:32

*Jb 36:18

*utriusque hominis sui

*cf. Csi 1:6

of crowds and entangled in cares, you would say that
he had been born for his country, not for himself.[228]
If you were to see him alone, living by himself, you
would have thought that he lived for God alone and
for himself.

¶4. Without being in the least disturbed he was involved in disturbance and confusion.[229] The time he
had dedicated to leisure he spent without leisure.[230]
How could he enjoy leisure when he was employed in
Ps 119:23   the justification of the Lord?* Although he had time
free from the needs of the people, nevertheless he
took no holiday from holy meditation or the pursuit
of prayer or even the very leisure of contemplation.
His conversation in that time of leisure was either
serious or there was none at all. His outward
appearance was either courteous or modest and kept
under control. To be sure—and this is a point of no
small praise among the learned—his eye was in his
Qo 2:14   head,* never flashing forth except when it was yield-
ing to power. His laughter either showed love or
elicited it, and even then it was rare. He did laugh
sometimes, but it was controlled and it so disclosed
the joy in his heart that his mouth did not lose but
cf. Lk 4:22   rather gained in grace.* It was so modest that he
could not be suspected of frivolity. It was so light
that it was sufficient to free his joyful countenance
Life ¶43   from every trace and cloud of sadness.* O perfect
Ps 20:3   gift! O fat burnt offering!* O pleasing service in mind
2 Co 2:15   and hand! How good to God* is the odor of the man
who spends his leisure in prayer! How good to men is
that of the man who exerts himself on their behalf!

1 Th 1:4, Si 45:1   ¶5. Because he was so beloved of God* and men,
therefore, Malachy was received this day, not un-
deservedly, into the company of the angels and
Life ¶12 & notes   became in fact what in name he was called.* He was
already an angel no less in purity than in name, but
the meaning of his glorious name is more happily
fulfilled in him now that he rejoices in equal glory and
happiness with the angels.[231] Most dearly beloved,
Jg 13:20   let us too rejoice that our angel ascended* to his

fellow-citizens, functioning as a legation for the
children of the captivity,* procuring for us the   *Dn 5:13, Ezr 4:1
sympathy of the blessed, impressing upon them the
longings of the wretched. Let us rejoice, I say, and be
glad,* that in the heavenly court there is someone   *Ps 118:24
who cares for us and by his merits protects us whom
he taught by his example and strengthened by his
miracles.

¶6. The holy bishop[232] who had often brought peace
offerings to the heavens in an humble spirit* has   *Dn 3:39, 87
by himself to the altar of God,* gone today himself   *Ps 43:4
the sacrifice and the priest. With the priest's passing,
the rite of sacrifice has been changed to something
better, the fountain of tears* has been dried up,   *Jr 9:1
every burnt sacrifice* is made with gladness and   *Lv 2:13, Mk 9:48
rejoicing.† Blessed be the Lord God* of Malachy,   †Ps 45:15
Who by the ministry of so great a bishop has visited   *Lk 1:68
his people and, now that he has been taken up into
the holy city,* does not cease to comfort our   *Mt 4:5
captivity* by the remembrance of such great sweet-   *cf. Ps 126: 1,4
ness. May the spirit of Malachy rejoice in the Lord,*   *Lk 1:47
for freed from the heavy burden of the body, he is
no longer weighed down by impure and earthly
matter. And thus passing through all creation, both
corporeal and incorporeal, with all eagerness and
liveliness, may he enter wholly into God and being
joined to Him may he be with Him one spirit
forever.*   *1 Co 6:17

¶7. Holiness becomes the house* in which the   *Ps 93:5
memory of such great sanctity† is celebrated. O   †Ps 30:4
Saint Malachy! keep it in holiness and justice,* having   *Lk 1:75
pity on us who ponder the memory of the abundance
of your sweetness* in the midst of so many and such   *Ps 145:6
great miseries. Great is the dispensation of God's
mercy on you who made yourself small in your own
eyes,* but great in his who did great things through   *1 S 15:17
you in saving your country and did great things for
you* in bringing you to his glory. May your festival,   *Lk 1:49
which is deservedly devoted to your virtues, benefit
our salvation by your merits and prayers. May the

*Ps 145:4

praise of your holiness* which we are celebrating be continued by the angels; thus it will be worthily pleasant for us if it should also be fruitful. As you go forth, may we who are gathered here today at this your delightful feast keep some remnants of the fruits of the Spirit with which you make your ascent so well laden.

*Dt 34:9
†2 K 2:9, 15
*Lk 1:17
†Si 45:6
*cf. Life ¶75

¶8. Be to us, we pray, another Moses* or another Elijah,† imparting to us something of your spirit; at least you have come in their spirit and power.* Your life, O Malachy, was a law of life and instruction,† your death the port of death and .the portal of life,* your memory the delight of gentleness and grace, your presence a crown of glory in the hand of the

*Is 62:3
†Ps 52:8
*Ps 45:7

Lord your God.* O fruitful olive tree in the house of God!† O oil of gladness,* anointing and enlightening, cherishing with favors, shining with miracles, make us participate in the light and the sweetness which you

*cf. Life ¶47

enjoy.* O fragrant lily ever blossoming and budding before the Lord and everywhere spreading a sweet

*Is 27:6,
Ho 14:6
†Si 45:1

and life-giving scent* whose memory among us is in benediction,† whose presence among those above is in honor. Grant to those who sing of you that they may not be defrauded of their share in so great an

*Si 24:2
†Ps 136:7
‡Jn 1:5
*Ps 46:4
†Si 50:6
*Si 50:6

assembly.* O great light† and light shining in the darkness,‡ lighting up the prison by the rays of signs and merits, making the city glad,* put to flight from our hearts the darkness of sin† by the brightness of your virtue. O morning star,* more brilliant than .the others, because you are closer to the day, more like the sun, deign to precede us that we too may walk

*1 Jn 1:7
†Eph 5:8
*Is 18:4

in the light* as children of light and not as children of darkness.† O dawn bringing day to the earth, but the noonday light* illuminating the highest reaches of heaven, receive us into the company of light, made bright by which you shed light far and wide and glow pleasantly within under the protection of our Lord Jesus Christ who with the Father and the Holy Spirit reigns God forever and ever. Amen.

I.

SAINT BERNARD'S
EPITAPH
ON SAINT MALACHY

I.

SAINT BERNARD'S
EPITAPH
ON SAINT MALACHY

A six-verse stanza in elegiac metre is to be found in a Vatican Library manuscript of some of the sermons of Saint Bernard having to do with Saint Malachy. It is here translated from SBOp 3:519-21.

There is no certainty that Saint Bernard composed this epitaph. But it has seemed well to include it here with his Life of Saint Malachy.

> *Do you wish to know who lies here?*
> *Dom Malachy.[1] Do you still insist? You came*
> *this far to ask who he was? An Irishman by*
> *homeland, holy in the performance of good*
> *acts; he was exalted in the working of mira-*
> *cles, held in honor as bishop. As legate of the*
> *Holy See he took on added duties. He was*
> *journeying to Rome, but he took flight to*
> *heaven from here.*

[1] *Domnus* 〉 *Dominus* designated an abbot in cistercian usage.

II.

SAINT BERNARD'S HYMN
IN HONOR OF SAINT MALACHY

II.

SAINT BERNARD'S HYMN
IN HONOR OF SAINT MALACHY

Some of the manuscripts of the works of Saint Bernard contain a hymn of ten quatrains in honor of Saint Malachy. The metre is a classical one, being Sapphic for three verses of each stanza and the fourth is a five syllable Adonic. In the judgment of such authorities as Dreves and Blume, we may accept these verses as the genuine work of Saint Bernard. They are here translated from SBOP 3:525-526.

1.
The bishop goes forth today, freed of his body,
Noble in signs, of sweet disposition,
A saint by his merits,
Famous in triumph.

2.
Nor does the name Malachy not suit the man,
Angel in meaning, like to the angels
In purity of life
Equal in glory.

3.

Our angel now given back to his own with the
Prayers of his confreres joined to the chorus.
  Exceeding many, equal to the best
  By his own merits.

4.

Moderate in living, chastity perpetual,
Faith and learning, the profit of souls,
  Mingling with Apostles
  Their equal in merits.

5.

Dutiful in action, virtuous in spirit,
Bishop and legate, he mastered them all.
  By this he brought honor
  Fairly on himself.

6.

If signs you seek, who could relate them?
This much I say: the dead woman risen
  Shows more than enough
  How great was his glory.

7.

Should Christ who reigns or we take much thought
Whom he loved first? He cared for the poor
  The lowly in spirit
  Humble as they are.

8.

Forbid, Lord, that he, the font of devotion
Should flow any the less, his dwelling now changed;
  Our father now blessed
  His orphans forsake!

9.

Your beloved Clairvaux, renowned for its treasure
Your body entombed. Pleading we pray for
  Your peace everlasting.
  Beloved Malachy.

10.
Glory to the Father and to the Son
And to the Spirit. One glory to all
Since all three are one
One majesty eternal.

ABBREVIATIONS

ABBREVIATIONS

AFM
: *Annals of the Four Masters* ed. J. O'Donovan. Dublin, 1851. 7 vols.

AI
: *Annals of Inisfallen* ed. Sean Mac Airt. Dublin, 1951.

ALC
: *Annals of Loch Cé* ed. W. M. Hennessy. London, 1871. 2 vols.

AU
: *Annals of Ulster* ed. W. M. Hennessy and B. McCarthy. Dublin, 1887-1901. 4 vols.

AA SS
: *Acta Sanctorum* a Bollandistis edita. Brussels, 1865.

CPT
: Cambridge Patristic Texts.

HSB
: Henry Bradshaw Society

ITS
: Irish Texts Society

James
: *The Letters of St. Bernard of Clairvaux newly translated* by B. S. James. Chicago, 1953.

Keating
: *History of Ireland,* trans. and ed. P. S. Dineen. London, 1912-1914. 4 vols.

Lawlor
: *St. Bernard of Clairvaux's Life of St. Malachy of Armagh,* trans. and ed. by H. J. Lawlor. London, 1920.

MGH
: Monumenta Germaniae Historica.

Missale Romanum	Rome, 1957
Onomasticon	E. Hogan, *Onomasticon Goedelicum locorum et tribuum Hiberniae et Scotiae.* Dublin, 1911.
PL	J. P. Migne. Patrologia Latina. Paris, 1844–65.
PRIA	Proceedings of the Royal Irish Academy, Dublin.
SLH	Scriptores Latini Hiberniae. Dublin.
VSH	*Vitae Sanctorum Hiberniae* ed. C. Plummer. Oxford, 1910. 2 vols.
Vacandard, E.	*Vie de Saint Bernard Abbé de Clairvaux.* Paris, 1927. 4th ed. 2 vols.

Scriptural citations are made using the
nomenclature and enumeration of The Jerusalem Bible.

NOTES

NOTES

THE LIFE OF SAINT MALACHY

1.   The *Life* was dedicated to Abbot Congan who had apparently asked Saint Bernard to give some account of the life of Malachy.

2.   Sg 2:12. Saint Bernard's own commentary on this passage *SC* 59:3 explains: The voice of the turtle 'is a sign that winter is past, proclaiming that the time of pruning has come . . . '. The voice, more like one who groans than one who sings admonishes us of our earthly pilgrimage. The quotation from Scripture occurs again in Bernard's letter to Pope Eugene III, a monk at Clairvaux before he became Pope: 'The voice of the turtle-dove has been heard in our chapter, and it has filled us with joy.' Ep 343 (James). The Benedictine edition listed it as letter 273.

3.   Abbot Congan to whom the *Life* is dedicated was a Cistercian as the words 'revered brother' imply. He is again mentioned *Life* 64.

4.   Saint Bernard is probably referring to Congan's own community of Cistercians. The word *ecclesia* means 'community' in *Life* 20.

5.   Saint Bernard makes a play on the words *educatus* and *edoctus*. This is a peculiarity of his style. On punning in the Church Fathers, see Leo Spitzer, *Linguistics and Literary History* (Princeton, 1948) 21, 35f.

6.   Bernard calls it *ventosa scientia*, 'windy' in the sense of 'puffed up, vain'. Behind this one may see Bernard taking a sly dig at the scholastic philosophers of his day, the *cimini sectores*, the 'hairsplitters' with whom he had very little sympathy. In this passage he is doubtless recalling how his own mother put him to school to learn holiness and to read and expound the Scriptures. (*Vita Bern*, c.2)

7.   From this it is apparent that Bernard did not know that Malachy's father was himself the teacher. AU a.1102 state that he was *ard fer legind*, 'a chief professor', at Armagh and died that year, when Malachy was about eight years old.

8.   We are told in *Vita Bern* c. 1 that Saint Bernard's mother refused to hand any of her children over to a wet-nurse, believing that children drew some of their goodness from their own mother whilst at the breast. Bernard places great stress upon Malachy's training at his mother's hand just as he himself had been educated by his mother Aleth.

9.   Ph 2:3. *inanem gloriam,* following the Vulgate which translated the Greek *kenodoxia,* often translated as *vana gloria,* 'vain-glory', one of the original eight capital sins. Cassian's *Institutes* still speaks of this original number, but by the time of Pope Gregory the Great (590-604) the number was reckoned as seven by amalgamating vainglory and pride into the single sin of pride. See Owen Chadwick, *John Cassian* (Cambridge, 1968, 2nd ed.) 42, 89, 94 f.

10.   This was Armagh (*Ir.* Ardmacha) the primatial see of all Ireland since the time of Saint Patrick. We are not told the name of the teacher.

11.   *retrahebat pedem, sistebat gradum.* This is a Vergilian reminiscense:

> *siste gradum,* teque aspectu ne *subtrahe* nostro
>
> *Aeneid* VI: 465.

12.   *Quid isti et illi?*—undoubtedly a reminiscence of the marriage feast at Cana (Jn 2:4) where Christ address Mary: 'Quid mihi et tibi est, mulier?'

13.   *viae et vitae huius:* See the Collect in the Mass for pilgrims and travellers: ut inter omnes *viae et vitae hujus* varietates . . . (*Missale Romanum,* Rome 1957) Missa votiva pro peregrinantibus et iter agentibus (86).

14.   This would be Imar O'Hagan founder of the monastery of Saint Peter and Saint Paul in Armagh. AU a. 1126 mention him as the abbot there. He died in Rome in 1134 according to the *Annals of the Four Masters.* Malachy mentions him as his teacher chap. 6, 8, 12, 14, 16.

15.   Some MSS say *hoc scit* for *hoc sit;* another says *aliter senserit.*

16.   Saint Bernard here makes a play on the words *conversio* and *conversatio.* In its technical sense *conversio* meant entry into a religious order, a turning towards God. Cassian tells us that both terms were used: *Conversatio (=vita monastica) et conversio erant ambo in usu communi, Contra Nestorium* 5.1. See further P. Delatte, *Commentary on the Rule of St. Benedict* tr. Dom Justin McCann (London, 1921, 1950) 367.

17.   This was Cellach, Archbishop of Armagh who died in 1129 (AU).

18.   In the roman rite of ordination, the ordaining prelate asks: 'Scis illos dignos esse?' (Do you know that they are worthy?) and the teacher must vouch for the intellectual and moral fitness of the candidate for the Sacred Order.

19.   In the Old Testament the members of the family of Levi were of the hereditary priesthood, but had not the power of the priests. They helped prepare the altar for sacrifice. In Late Latin *levita=diaconus,* a grade in Holy Orders immediately below the priesthood.

20.   Deacons were ordained for service, not only for liturgical functions, but to help in charitable work in the christian community. In burying the dead Saint Malachy was carrying out one of the corporal works of mercy. Not only did he decently bury the dead body, once the

temple of the Holy Spirit, but he performed a humanitarian function in that the presence of many unburied bodies would soon lead to an outbreak of sickness, especially in those days when hygiene and medicines were not generally available. Eusebius, HE 7.11.24 tells of a deacon at Alexandria in Egypt who helped bury martyrs in the persecution of Valerian in the third century. The office was a dangerous one and the deacon, also named Eusebius, later became Bishop of Laodicea (ibid.).

21.   Saint Bernard means that Malachy's sister quotes Sacred Scripture correctly, but she makes the wrong application.

22.   Literally 'that the priestly office be conferred upon him'. Apparently it was Bishop Cellach and Imar who saw him performing so well in his diaconal role, which in those days was the practical training for the priest and normally covered a period of five years.

23.   This would have been about 1119. Various church Councils regulated the minimum age at which deacons and priests could be ordained. The Council of Melfi 1089 set the diaconate at 24 or 25 years of age and the priesthood at 30, but the Council of Ravenna (1315) lowered the age to 20 and 25 respectively.

24.   The Irish Church was apt to disregard the canons of continental councils, but not as a deliberate act of disobedience. We must take into account the condition of the times, the difficulty of travel, etc. It would appear that Bernard himself was ordained a priest at twenty-five and this would have been a century before the Council of Ravenna which lowered the age limit.

25.   See Mt 25:14-29, Lk 19:12-26, the Parable of the Talents. Cellach was elected Bishop of Dublin in 1121 according to the *Annals of Ulster*. Apparently he entrusted his diocese to Malachy when he departed for his new see.

26.   *plantationes malas,* which Lawlor translates 'evil plantings' with a reference to Saint Ignatius of Antioch, *Epistle to the Trallians,* 11. Cassian, *Collationes* 18,7,1 speaks of *noxia illa plantatio.*

27.   According to Keating (III.297-317), a Synod was convened in Ireland at Raith Bresail in 1100 by order of Gilla Easpuig (Gillespie), the bishop of Limerick who was the Pope's legate in Ireland at that time. They made regulations and customs for the church and the laity and defined diocesan boundary lines more accurately.

28.   *Malachias de novo instituit . . .* Are we to understand *de novo* 'anew' to mean that such had been the previous custom but had died out for a long time? I believe so, since the word *primum* would have been used if Malachy had been the first to introduce such usages.

29.   Malchus is the Latinized form of Mael Isa Ua h-Ainmire. AFM II:1049 mentions his death as Bishop of Waterford in 1135. Malchus was about 75 years old when Malachy visited him.

30.   Bernard here distinguishes Scots and Irish. In the earlier Middle Ages *Scotia* was Ireland, and the *Scoti* were the Irish. Some traces of this remain in this *Life:* in ¶14 an oratory is spoken of as a Scotic

work (*opus Scoticum*). In ¶72 Ireland is called 'further Scotland' (*ulterior Scotia*).

31.   It was called a celebrated place because of its monastic discipline and the holy lives led there.

32.   Some of the MSS omit *australis* in the first instance, but these are the ones which add it in the next phrase, reading 'Munster which is the southern part of Ireland . . . ' (*pars australis*).

33.   AI a.1124 say that Tadg, son of Mac Carthaig, king of Cashel, died. The other Annals say that he was king of Desmond (South Munster) which is more likely. His son Cormac succeeded him as king.

34.   *Necessitatem in virtutem convertit*: this is a proverbial expression. See Saint Jerome, *Adv. Rufinum* 3.2: *Habeo gratiam quod facis de necessitate virtutem*; Chaucer, *Knight's Tale*, 3042: 'To maken vertu of necessitee,' etc.

35.   I believe that modern physiology has proven that cold baths are more apt to urge lustful feelings as a reaction once the warm blood flowed back.

36.   The neighboring king was Conor O'Brien of North Munster (Tuadmumu, Eng. Thomond).

37.   This was the biblical Judas Maccabaeus, leader of the Jewish resistance to foreign tyranny.

38.   *effractor* does not occur in classical Latin. Latham, *Revised Medieval Latin Word-List for British and Irish Sources* (London, 1965) p. 161, cites it as first found in the early twelfth century.

39.   This was Bangor in Northern Ireland near present day Belfast. The town still remains. The Irish form *Bennchor* is explained by a folk-etymology as 'White Choir' or even 'Choir of Women'.

40.   . . . *sua omnia dedit, et se quoque*. He accepted Malachy's rule in the new community.

41.   As in Classical Latin *avunculus* meant the mother's brother. This was Muirchertach Ua h-Innechtaig, who died in 1131 (AFM).

42.   Malachy (L. Malachias) probably assumed his name when he became abbot of Bangor: his name was *Mael Maedoc*. An old Latin Life of Saint Patrick, attributed to Jocelin, relates that when Patrick visited Comgall's monastery of Bangor he said it was 'filled with a multitude of the heavenly host'. Hence it was called *Vallis Angelorum* and it was so known in the early seventeenth century. Malachy may have taken his name from the legend, for *Malachiae* is a latinized form of the Hebrew *Mala'âki* 'my angel'. See Msgr Albert Vincent, *Lexique Biblique* (Tournai, 1961) 311. Saint Bernard dwelt upon this in his Sermon (2.5) on an anniversary of Malachy's death.

43.   There is a Latin life of Saint Comgall edited by Plummer in VSH II.1-21. See especially chap. 13 'Constituitque magnum monasterium, quod vocatur Beannchor, in regione quae dicitur altitudo Ultorum, iuxta mare orientale. Et maxima multitudo monachorum ibi venit ad sanctum Comgallum, ut non potuissent esse in uno loco. Et

inde plurimas cellas et multa monasteria, non solum in regione Ultorum sed per alias Hiberniae provincias construxit.' Comgall, born between 516 and 520, was a Pict of the Dal Araide. He founded the monastery of Bangor about 559 and died in 602 (AU).

44. Lugaid or Mo-Lua, here latinized as Luanus, was the founder of the Monastery of Lismore in Scotland. The *Annals of Ulster* record his death as 592. He is commemorated on 25 June in the *Martyrologies* of Oengus, Tallaght, and Gorman (HBS XXIX.158; LXVIII.52; IX.122). The Aberdeen Breviary contains a life (*Breviarium Aberdonense: Pars aestivalis, Prop. Sanctorum,* fol. 5ᵛ-7. Edinburgh, 1854), in the readings for 25 June. He is probably the bishop who ordained Saint Comgall and prevailed upon him to remain in Ireland when he wished to go to Britain (See Plummer, VSH I.lix; II.6-7).

45. Bernard here continues his rhetorical figure of the growth and spread of the monastic foundations.

46. Saint Columbanus was perhaps the greatest of the Irish missionaries in continental Europe. Born in Leinster about 430, he embraced the monastic life at Bangor in its early days. There he must have received a good classical education as his poems, letters and homilies show an acquaintance with many ancient authors. He left Ireland about 590, in his old age, as he tells us, and went to France, founding the Abbey of Luxeuil. He was driven out of France by a local king and went over the Alps to North Italy. On the way one of his disciples, Saint Gall, became ill and stayed behind in Switzerland. His hermitage became the foundation of the great Abbey of Saint Gall, a stronghold of piety and learning in the early Middle Ages. In 612 Columbanus founded the Abbey of Bobbio in Lombardy, where he died in 615 on 23 November. A good life written by Jonas of the Bobbio community in the next generation is still extant in many manuscripts. It is valuable since Jonas got his information from Columbanus' own contemporaries. It was edited by B. Krusch in MGH *Script. rerum Meroving.* (1902) IV,1-152 and the *editio minor* for the use of students (Leipzig, 1905). See also H.J. Lawlor, 'The manuscripts of the Vita S. Columbani' TRIA 32, Sec. C. Pt. 1 (Dublin, 1903). The works of Columbanus are edited and translated into English by G. S. M. Walker, *Sancti Columbani Opera* (Dublin, 1957) [SLH vol. II].

47. Gn 12:2, 46:3. Luxeuil was some eighty miles from Clairvaux and well known to Saint Bernard. Fifty years after Columbanus' death the harsh celtic monastic rule there was replaced by that of Saint Benedict. It continued to 1789, when it was suppressed by the French government. See Margaret Stokes, *Three Months in the Forests of France: a Pilgrimage in search of Vestiges of the Irish Saints in France* (London, 1895) 45-70, for an account of the abbey and the destruction of the library in 1789.

48. The monastery of Bangor was laid waste by the Norsemen in 824, according to the *Annals of Ulster*: 'The plundering of the monastery of Bangor by foreigners (Gaill and Norsemen) and the despoiling of its

oratory. The relics of Saint Comgall were scattered out of their reliquary.' AI adds to this that its 'learned men and bishops were slain with the sword.' (AI 125).

49.   Whether this refers to 824 or to a later raid in 958 (AU I.475) when 'Tanaidhe son of Odhar, coarb of Bangor, was killed by foreigners,' the number of the slain is certainly exaggerated. Where did Bernard himself get this information which is mentioned in no Irish annals? The editors of the critical edition of St Bernard's works have a note here that the information may have come from some of Malachy's own monks who stayed on in Clairvaux after his death.

50.   At the time of the Dissolution in 1539, the holdings of Bangor included thirty-four townlands, along with nine rectories or chapels and their tithes. (N. M. Archdall, *Monasticon Hibernicum*, ed. P. F. Moran I (1873) 235.

51.   Between 824 and 1123 the *Annals of Ulster* mention twenty abbots or coarbs of Bangor. But a certain Indrechtach who died in 906 is the last to bear the title of abbot. (AU I.421).

52.   Early Irish and Anglo-Saxon churches were built of wood and the introduction of building with stone was due to roman influence. Bede, HE III.25, mentions that Finan built a wooden church at Lindisfarne: *fecit ecclesiam . . . more Scottorum, non de lapide, sed de robore secto totam composuit.* (ed. Plummer [Oxford, 1956] II.101). For a discussion of early churches in Ireland, see George Petrie, *The Ecclesias-Architecture of Ireland . . . comprising an essay on the Origin and Uses of the Round Towers of Ireland* (Dublin, TRIA 20 (1845) 138-151.

53.   This was Imar O'Hagan who founded the monastery of Saint Paul and Saint Peter at Armagh and built a *stone church* there which was consecrated on 21 October 1126. He died in 1134 and is mentioned in Gorman's *Martyrology* on 13 August. Malachy always considered him his master. See ¶¶ 5, 6, 8, 12, 14, 16.

54.   Christian, whose Irish name was Gille Criost Ua Conairche, was a disciple of Saint Malachy and visited Clairvaux with him in 1139. With some companions he was left there to learn the cistercian way of life as it was practised at Clairvaux by Bernard and his community. Later he became Abbot of Mellifont (1152) and Bishop of Lismore. See Columcille Conway, OCSO, *The Story of Mellifont* (Dublin, 1958).

55.   Bernard knew that the ties of religion could be stronger than mere blood relationships. In his Commentary on the Canticle of Canticles (26.4) he bemoans his recently departed brother Gerard: 'He was my brother by blood, yet more my brother in religion.'

56.   See ¶ 68. This is present-day Soulseat, some eight miles from Cairngarroch. The Cistercians named the place *Stagnum Viride* (Green Lake).

57.   The city is apparently Connor, but Bernard was mistaken in saying that it was near Bangor. It is about twenty-five miles distant.

58.   This was the see of Connor which included Bangor within its

jurisdiction. The Synod of Rathbreasail in 1110 defined the boundaries of the Irish dioceses. See Keating, *History* 3:303.

59. Imar was apparently approached to sway Malachy when the others' entreaties were of no avail.

60. AFM 1124: 'St. Maelmaedhog O'Morgair sat in the bishopric of Connor.'

61. The term 'athlete of Christ, of the Lord, of God' occurs often, beginning with the Apostolic Fathers. See *A Patristic Greek Lexicon* ed. G. W. H. Lampe (Oxford, 1961) 46, for the Greek Fathers, and A. Blaise, 102, for the Latin. Bernard might have had the phrase from either Saint Augustine or Cassian as a source, but there is a strong possibility that he might have had it from a Latin translation of the Ignatian Epistles. An early Latin translation of the Letters of Saint Ignatius of Antioch exists in manuscripts, most of them of Burgundian provenance, and among them a Clairvaux manuscript of the twelfth century which Bernard may have used. In that Latin version the term *athleta Dei* occurs in the *Letter to Polycarp*, 2.3 and again in the *Letter to Hero, Deacon of Antioch* 1. See also J. H. Petermann, *S. Ignatii Patris Apostolici quae feruntur Epistolae . . . collatis edd. Graecis, versionibusque Syriaca, Armeniaca, Latinis . . .* (Leipzig, 1849) 266, 376.

62. Bernard uses much the same language in the *De consideratione* addressed to Pope Eugene III, formerly a monk at Clairvaux. 'They were sheep and turned into wolves; why despair of their turning back again into sheep?' (trans. G. Lewis [Oxford, 1918] 103.) Csi 4:6; SBOp 3:453, CF 37:116-117.

63. 2 M 15:21. The Irish called this *cross-figil,* praying with arms extended in the form of a cross, a customary monastic practice. It is mentioned in the Old Irish Penitentials. See L. Bieler–D. A. Binchy, *The Irish Penitentials* [SLH 5] (Dublin, 1963) 365. VSH I. cxx, n.1; Bede, HE 2:269 f.

64. *erogabat, vel ingratis, caelestis tritici mensuram.* In old roman law the word *erogo* meant 'to pay money out of the public treasury.' Here in a specialized sense it means 'to give even to the undeserving what was their heritage, the Bread from heaven.'

65. The City was Bangor and the time may have been 1130, when Connor O'Loughlin subdued Ulster. Both the *Annals of Ulster* and those of Loch Cé mention that he was murdered 25 May 1136.

66. Armagh has been the seat of the Primate of Ireland since the time of Saint Patrick in the fifth century.

67. Connor O'Brien was king of Thomond (North Munster) and Cormac Mac Carthy king of Desmond (South Munster). See note 36.

68. According to Colgan, *Trias Thaumaturga* (Louvain, 1647) 301, we are not to understand 'generation' as the life span of an individual, but rather the period of office of successive coarbs. AU mention six bishops of Armagh contemporary with lay abbots.

69. From the very earliest times there was the symbolism of marriage

between a bishop and his diocese. In that sense bishops could be considered 'adulterous' who took charge of their sees unjustly (by uncanonical means). So in ¶21, Malachy refers to his former diocese as his 'spouse'. Bernard here refers to the depraved custom (*ius pravum*) of bishops claiming their sees on the basis of family descent rather than spiritual fitness.

70.   AU a. 1111 reported that fifty bishops attended the Synod of Fiadh meic Oengusa, most of them from Ulster and Munster.

71.   The Latin form of the name was Celsus. He is mentioned in AU a. 1129 where his burial at Lismore is recorded. Some of the manuscripts here read *Celestinum* for *Celsum*.

72.   AU a. 1129 record that Cellach died on 1 April, was buried on 4 April and the next day Murtough was appointed coarb.

73.   AFM a.1136 report that it was very probably Conor O'Loughlin, who was king of Oriel where Armagh was situated. The five year period was actually five and one-half years as he died September 17, 1134.

74.   This was Mael Isa Ua h-Ainmire called Malchus in Latin. See ¶8. He had been a monk of Winchester before being called to Lismore as bishop. He must have been about 85 years of age at this time.

75.   Gillebertus, a latinization of *Gilla espuig* 'servant of the bishop', hence the surname Gillespie. He signed the Acts of the Synod of Ráthbreasail using the Irish form of his name according to Keating, III:306. He was a great friend of St Anselm, Arch. of Canterbury, 1093-1109.

76.   He was already bishop of Connor.

77.   The spouse was the diocese of Connor. In the sermon delivered by Saint Bernard on the day of Malachy's death he mentioned the whole episode (I.6). It is said that after he ordained his successor, once the troubles in Armagh were resolved, he lived a life of voluntary poverty in the Diocese of Connor, refusing ecclesiastical and secular revenues, living as a simple monk and refusing to have even personal property for himself.

78.   *mulier procerae staturae et reverendi vultus.* See Boethius, *Consolatio Philosophiae,* I, Pr.1: *mulier reverendi admodum vultus* (ed, A. Fortescue [London, 1925] 2).

79.   AFM a. 1133 report that Mauricius made a visitation of Tir Eoghain (counties of Derry and Tyrone) receiving his tribute of cows and giving his blessing. Apparently according to this entry Malachy did not cover the entire province in his ministrations.

80.   Bernard makes a pun upon the name Nigellus which would be a diminutive of *niger,* 'black'. He probably refers more to his character rather than to a bodily characteristic. On punning in the Church Fathers, see Leo Spitzer, *Linguistics and Literary History* (Princeton, 1948) 21, 35 f.

81.   Maurice would insure that others would continue to be damned, because he appointed Nigellus who would drag them into hell along with

him. This seems a very strong statement coming from the gentle Saint Bernard. The reference is to the Gideonites mentioned in the history of Joshua, chapter nine. They had arranged a strategem by which they should live on instead of being killed with the Canaanites.

82. Niall was a cousin to Maurice and brother of Cellach.

83. *vicinamque elementa intenta omnia mortem.* A reminiscence of of Vergil, *Aeneid* I.91: *praesentemque viris intentant omnia mortem*, ed. J. W. Mackail (Oxford, 1930).

84. AFM a.1134 record this entry. Malachy was probably forty years of age at that time, having entered his province in his thirty-eighth year. Bernard may have misunderstood his sources.

85. Ws 3:1. *qui remanent in manu Dei,* 'he remains in the hand of God,' a pun on the words *maneo/manus,* a frequent stylistic device in Saint Bernard's writings.

86. The Old Irish Penitentials considered it a sacrilege to steal the Book of Gospels from a church or any other signs of office. See Bieler–Binchy, *Old Irish Penitentials* (SLH 5 [Dublin, 1963] 267). This is the celebrated Book of Armagh which is now in the Trinity College, Dublin, library. It contains not only the Latin text of the Gospels and the Epistles, but also memoranda for a Life of Saint Patrick and Sulpicius Severus' Life of Saint Martin of Tours. Both these saints were accounted worthy to be recorded in the Gospel book, both of them having been missionaries and equals of the Apostles themselves. See the splendid edition of this book edited by Prof. John Gwynn (Dublin, 1913). Popular tradition connected it with Saint Patrick but this is impossible.

87. Only Saint Bernard mentions that this crozier was fashioned by Christ. Giraldus Cambrensis (thirteenth century) in his *Topography of Ireland* 3:34, describes it as a wooden crozier richly adorned. The *Tripartite Life of St. Patrick* edited by W. Stokes (London, 1887) p. 30, says that it was given by Christ to Saint Patrick. This is a tenth century source which embodies earlier traditions. AU a.788 mention that it was profaned and it was regarded as the principal relic of Saint Patrick. AFM 1135 state that Malachy 'purchased the *bachall Isa* and took it from its cave'. Are we to assume from this that Niall had hidden it away after stealing it? It was taken to Christ Church Cathedral in Dublin sometime in the late twelfth century, and ALC a.1538 say that it was destroyed by the English in that year. For the *baculum Jesu* see AA SS Martii II, pp. 541 ff.

88. This may have been some local chieftain, and the king who is here mentioned must have been Connor O'Brien.

89. Bernard means that as Christ has shared in our humanity by taking human form, He has sanctified the body of man. What a privilege, says Saint Malachy, to offer that body back to Christ in martyrdom.

90. ut *calcato limine* domus: See Apuleius, *Metamorphoses* 11:23

. . . et *calcato* Proserpinae *limine* . . . (ed. R. Helm [Leipzig, 1931] 285.14).

91.   terribil*iter multatum in corpore* . . . . misericord*iter mutatum in corde:* this stylistic device cannot be reproduced in English.

92.   This was the church at Armagh, not the Church Universal!

93.   This could be a corruption of some name or other. Nothing is known of such a person except this mention by.Bernard here. Many of the important manuscripts of the *Life* omit the name entirely.

94.   This was Gilla mac Liag mac Ruaidri, formerly abbot of Saint Columba in Derry. He was transferred to Armagh in 1137 (AFM) and died in 1174 (AU).

95.   *ad suam parochiam redit.* The diocese of a bishop was spoken of as his parish.

96.   Sg 1:14, 5:12. The *Vita Prima* of Saint Bernard tells us that he had 'dove-like eyes,' (V. 12) meaning a 'certain angelic purity shining in his eyes and a dove-like simplicity'.

97.   See Adam of Perseigne, Ep 10: *Ad Sancti Martini Cultores;* SCh 66:164, CF 21:140, where Saint Martin of Tours is likened to the Apostles. See also Odo of Cluny in his hymn to Saint Martin: '*Martine, par Apostolis* . . . ' (Dreves-Blume, *Ein Jahrtausend Lateinischer Hymnendichtung* [Leipzig, 1909] I.120.) and Adam of Saint Victor in his hymn *Gaude Sion, quae diem recolis/qua Martinus, compar Apostolis* . . . *(Oeuvres poétiques,* ed. L. Gautier, [Paris, 1894]) 210.

98.   The *pallium* worn by an archbishop had been considered since the eleventh century as a sign of the 'fulness of the pontifical office'.

99.   This was the See of Cashel where the kings of Munster reigned. As early as the year 1110, when the Council of Rathbreasail was held, Malchus signed himself Archbishop of Cashel. See Keating, *History* III:306.

100.   The trip to Rome in those days took about nine months. Malachy may not have been in good health at that time.

101.   His Irish name was Gille Criost Ua Morgair. His predecessor, Cinaeth Hua Baigill, died in 1135 according to the *Annals of Tigernach* (ed, W. Stokes, *Revue Celtique* 18 [Paris, 1897] 153). Apparently he became Bishop of Clogher that year, and died in 1138. He was buried in the Church of SS Peter and Paul in Armagh according to AFM II. 1059.

102.   Mediaeval canon law considered that a bishop was married to his diocese. The bishop's ring then as now was a symbol of this espousal.

103.   We could not expect Bernard to be familiar with the route which Malachy took, but an attempt has been made by the Rev. H. J. Lawlor in his 'Notes on St. Bernard's Life of St. Malachy,' PRIA 35 (Dublin, 1919) 238-243.

104.   Sycarus was the latinization of the Old English name *Sighere.* He was a priest of Newbald in the Diocese of York, mentioned by

Jocelin in his *Vita S. Waltheni* (AA SS Aug I:255. Between 1126-30 he wrote the *Vita et Visio Orm Simplicis* edited now by H. Farmer in *Anal. Boll.* 75 (Brussels, 1957) 72-82.

105. Malachy left some of his own monks with Bernard at Clairvaux so that they might learn of the cistercian way of life. Some of this group later founded Mellifont Abbey in Ireland. See ¶ 39.

106. *ad discendam conversationis formam.* This is the *conversio morum* of the Benedictine Rule, implying a complete re-orientation of one's way of life upon assuming the religious habit. It was the *metanoia*, the 'turning back', of the Desert Fathers. See E. Gilson, *The Mystical Theology of Saint Bernard,* trans. A. H. C. Downes (New York, 1955) 43, 79, 135, 150. (*La Théologie mystique de Saint Bernard* [Paris, 1947] 61, 102 f., 158, 175).

107. Wallenus in the Latin text may be a scribal error for Wallevus, son of King David I of Scotland. He entered the Cistercian Order, having been prior of the Augustinian Canons at Kirkham and became abbot of Melrose in 1148, the year of Malachy's death. There is a life by Jocelin in AA AS Aug I:248.

108. *Runcinus* is a Mediaeval Latin word not found before the late eleventh century, with the meaning 'stallion, hack, pack horse'. Through the Old French *roncin* we have English *rouncy*. The Shipman in Chaucer also had a hard time of it riding his rouncy:

> He rood upon a rouncy, as he kouthe.
> *Canterbury Tales,* 390.

(*Works of Geoffrey Chaucer* ed. F.N. Robinson [Boston, 1957[2]] 21.

109. *Palefridus* was a corruption of Late Latin *paraveredus*, 'pack horse', found in Cassiodorus, *Variae* 5:39; 11:14 (PL 69:672D, 840C. *Palefridus* through the Old French gave us English *palfrey,* but the form *paraveredus* gave German *Pferd.*

110. According to Jocelin's account in AA SS, this took place in a few days.

111. See Preface, ¶ 2. Here Saint Bernard notes the beginning of his acquaintance with Malachy, which would have been probably 1139.

112. Malachy apparently left the main route on his way to Rome at Bar-sur-Aube some eight miles distant from Clairvaux. Most of his retinue must have travelled by foot and would welcome a few days' rest on their tedious journey.

113. *intimis visceribus colligens:* this must be a Scriptural or patristic reminiscence. Ancient Hebrew symbolism made the bowels the seat of the affections; note the phrase *per viscera misericordiae* in the *Benedictus* canticle (Lk 1:78).

114. This is the present day Ivrea in North Italy, the meeting place of two routes across the Alps, the Great Saint Bernard and the Little Saint Bernard. In classical times it was named Eporedia and the name is mentioned in Tacitus, *Histories* 1:70 (ed. Rev. W.A. Spooner [London, 1891] 171). It is an old Celtic place-name.

115. *lucris potius uberioribus:* not profitable in a worldly sense. The Pope (*vir Apostolicus,* Bernard calls him) believed that as Bishop of Armagh and Primate of all Ireland Malachy exercised a greater sphere of spiritual influence than he would have as a simple monk at Clairvaux.

116. The *Vita Prima* 7.4 uses the same words of the Swedish people. See also Vacandard II:416. But the term *gentes* may here simply mean 'tribes' as in ¶42, where Bernard is speaking of Irish tribes, not foreign nations.

117. *a latere suo* lit. 'from his side', meaning one who was intimate with him.

118. Ep 383 of Bernard to Malachy mentions receiving other candidates for the monastic life and remarks that they are all doing well and that he will not send a similar group until he feels that they are well trained in the spiritual life (James, 452-453).

119. This was Gilla Crist ua Condoirche, possibly one of those left at Clairvaux on Malachy's return from Rome. He was the first Abbot of Mellifont, but his rule was not successful. He was later consecrated Bishop of Lismore and he appeared as apostolic legate at the Synod of Kells in 1152 (Keating, 3:317). According to ALC he died in 1186.

120. At least twelve fully professed religious were required canonically to constitute an abbey.

121. It should be noted here that this is the only *prophecy* of Malachy mentioned by Bernard. The so-called 'Prophecies of Malachy' are a late forgery.

122. Aelred of Rievaulx, another Cistercian, has this to say of Henry: ' . . . David had a son Henry, a man gentle and pious, a man of sweet nature and of pure heart, and worthy in all things to be born of such a father. And with him I have lived from the cradle, and have grown up with him as boys together; and in my youth I have known his youth also. And in the body, but never in mind or affection, in order to serve Christ I left him, in the full bloom of his prime . . . . ' (tr. A. O. Anderson, *Scottish Annals from English Chroniclers* [London, 1908] 156).

123. A town in the parish of Sorby in Wigtownshire.

124. This must be the present Kirk Mochrum some twelve miles from Cruggleton. In those days a small village gathered around a church took the name of the church for its identification.

125. *Portus Lapasperi,* a corrupt form for *Lapidis asperi* gen. sg. of *Lapis asper,* 'rough stone', which is a Latin translation of the Scotch-Gaelic *carn garbh* which means 'rough stone'. There are three places on the shore of Wigtownshire bearing the name Cairngarbh. From there the Bangor coast could be well seen on a clear day.

126. Many such structures have been found in western Wales. The interwoven twigs and branches formed a wall which was then daubed over with clay and allowed to harden into a solid wall.

127. From the canonical viewpoint it seems highly irregular that Malachy should not only erect an oratory but also consecrate a cemetery

in someone else's territory. Of course, he may have had permission to do so, but I believe that Saint Bernard wishes to stress the point here that Malachy being delayed several days could not stand by idly, but saw the need for an oratory for himself and his retinue for even those few days.

128. 'Non destitit ille, *furiis agitatus iniquis.*' In this perfect hexameter rhythm Bernard combined lines from two classical Latin poets:

conuingis et scelerum *Furiis agitatus* Orestes
(Vergil, *Aeneid* 3:331)
Et quoniam in patria, fatis *agitatus iniquis*
(Ovid, *Ars Amoris* 2:27)

129. Lawlor did not translate this episode but he did print the Latin text in his appendix, p. 171.

130. See Saint Bernard's sermon on the first anniversary of the passing of Malachy II:3: 'He made no distinction of sex or age or condition of person.'

131. The *Vita Prima* of Saint Bernard says the same thing about himself. (3:1) As Leclercq points out in the critical edition, a part of this eulogy of Saint Malachy was also taken over by Gerlach of Milwick in his life of Godschalk, *Continuatio annalium Vincentii Pragensis* (MGH Scriptores 17:700, 23-36).

132. See Bernard's sermon of 2 November 1149 (II:4) for a similar description of Malachy's personal qualities.

133. See also the consecration prayer in the ordination of deacons in the Gelasian and Gregorian Sacramentaries, *Orationes ad ordinandum diaconun: Consecratio (Le Sacramentaire Grégorien* . . . Spicilegium Friburgenses, vol. 16, ed. Jean Deshusses [Friburg, 1971] p. 98).

134. The word *paruchia* means diocese in this context rather than parish. As legate Malachy was free to move all about Ireland. See n. 95.

135. See Bernard, *De diligendo Deo* VII:17: 'Paul did not preach the Gospel that he might eat, but he ate that he might preach the Gospel; for he loved not food, but the Gospel.' Cf. CF 19:110.

136. *altaria cumulet.* See the Secret Prayer of the Mass for the Nativity of Saint John the Baptist (June 24): 'Tua, Domine, muneribus *altaria cumulamus* . . . ' (*Missale Romanum* [Rome, 1957] 586).

137. Illi plebes ne agnoscunt quidem . . . . In the twelfth century Lat. *plebs* no longer meant 'common people, the horde' as in classical times, but 'laity, congregation, parishoner', as distinct from the clerical state.

138. Quid ergo *mirum,* si *mira* est operatus, sic *mirabilis* ipse?

139. Coleraine still exists in County Derry, North Ireland. In early times it had a monastery there which was said to have been founded by Saint Patrick.

140. Saint Bernard lists some of Malachy's miracles by type rather than in strictly chronological order. The first four have to do with the expelling of demons (¶¶45-46).

141. This is Fir Li which included the barony of Coleraine. See

Edmund Hogan, *Onomasticon Goedelicum* . . . (Dublin, 1910) 482.

142. In the *Vita Sancti Galli* by Walafrid Strabo there is reported a similar conversation between the demon of the water and the demon of the mountain (chapter 7). See Maud Joynt, *The Life of St. Gall* (London, S.P.C.K., 1927 [Translations of Christian Literature. Series V: Lives of Celtic Saints]) 72-73.

143. Here are related three instances of Saint Malachy curing the insane.

144. Ulidia at the time of Malachy was the region of eastern Ulster which comprises at the present time the counties of Down and part of Antrim. It was there that Saint Patrick made his first convert.

145. This begins a new list of three miracles curing mutes.

146. Oenthreb in the MSS also occurs in Old Irish texts as Aenthreb, or even Aentruimh as an older form of the name Antrim.

147. See Saint Bernard's sermon preached on the first anniversary of Malachy's death, chap. 8.

148. Cluenvania, but some MSS have Duenvania where originally *cl-* was mistaken for *d-* something which could happen only in Latin MSS. It was the Old Irish Cluain Uama 'Meadow of the Cave' in present-day County Cork.

149. This was Nehemiah Moriarty who died in 1149 (AFM II:1087): In the *Vision of Tundale* he is said to be one of four bishops who are with Saint Patrick in Paradise—Malachy, Cellach, and Christian O'Mogair being the others. See *Tundale: das mittelenglische Gedicht über die Vision des Tundals* . . . ed. A. Wagner (Halle, 1893) 125-127.

150. Lawlor thought that Saint Bernard might have learned this story from Marcus, the author of the *Vision of Tundale* written in 1149. See V. H. Friedel-K. Meyer, *La Vision de Tondale* . . . (Paris, 1907) vi-xii.

151. *cum comite.* Saint Bernard is mistaken here in applying a frankish feudal title to an Irish chieftain. There were no *counts* in Ireland until after the Anglo-Norman invasion late in the twelfth century.

152. There were neither knights, counts, nor squires in Ireland at the time of Malachy. Bernard did not realize that the feudal system had not extended to Ireland. This happened only after the Norman invasion, long after both Malachy and Bernard were dead.

153. This may have been Dermot Mac Murrough who ruled as King of Leinster, 1126-1171. When driven from his kingdom in 1166, he invited the Anglo-Normans to help him and Ireland was afterwards subject to Norman rule. There is an Anglo-Norman poem about this ascribed to Morice Regan who was *latimer* or secretary to Dermot and was the interpreter to the incoming Normans. It has been edited with an English translation by G. H. Orpen: *The Song of Dermot and the Earl* (Oxford, 1892). The manuscript lacks the first folio and so is without a title which may have been *La Chanson de Dermot,* or *La Chanson de Dermot et le Conte.*

154. This and the following two miracles have to do with the

healing of paralytics.

155. Young boys offered to the monastic community were called *oblates* (*oblatus* fr. *offero*). Such boys, very often younger sons, were entrusted to a monastery for safe-keeping and education. Many of them later entered the community as novices. Should they return to the world later on, they were generally better-educated than most and became the secretaries of feudal lords or professional scribes.

156. Saint Finbarr, patron saint of Cork, founded a monastery there in the sixth century. AFM 2:1063 mentions that Donnell Shalvey erenach of Cork died in 1040. This may have caused the vacancy.

157. Lk 17:18. This appears to have been Giolla Aodha O Maighin who is reported in Keating's *History* (3:317) as having attended the Synod of Kells in 1152. He had been a monk at Errew in present day County Mayo, hence he was an outsider (*alienigena*) and a poor man (*pauper*) because being a religious he was vowed to poverty in worldly goods. AU (2:173) and AFM (3:3) give the date of his death as 1172.

158. Now follow three miracles of Malachy having to do with women, one very sick, another dead, and a third spiritually dead.

159. Here follow two incidents having to do with a miraculous draught of fish.

160. Faughart is two miles west of Dundalk according to Hogan, *Onomasticon Goedelicum,* 426 and the parish church of St Brigid is there.

161. The fourth *Vita* of Saint Brigid likewise makes Faughart her birthplace. See Colgan, *Trias Thaumat.* 547 (*Vita* 1:6). The Old Irish life in Oxford, Bodl. Rawl. B.512 which lacks the first folio, tells of her miracles partly in Latin, partly Irish, and c. 28 may possibly refer to Faughart, where she healed two paralytics: 'duas virgines paraliticas *Fotharenses*'. Bernard gives the Irish form of the name as Fochairt. See *Irish Texts* edited by J. Fraser, P. Grosjean SJ, and J. G. O'Keeffe, Fasc. I (London, 1931): *Vitae Brigitae,* 2-18, edited by Charles Plummer who died in 1926.

162. This would have been the Kilcurry River.

163. *sciolus:* a Late Latin word meaning 'one who is learned in his own estimation, a show-off, a pedant, one who has little organized knowledge'. Hence English *sciolist* 'a know-nothing'.

164. This unnamed cleric may have been a follower of Berengarius who retracted his heretical teachings regarding the Eucharist at the sixth Roman Council in 1079. See Mansi 20:524D; Denzinger, *Enchiridion* (14-18 ed. 1922) c.355. He had been condemned by Leo IX in the Roman Council of 1050, by Pope Victor II at the Synod of Florence in 1055; by Pope Nicholas II in the Roman Synod of 1059; and by Pope Gregory VII in both councils at Rome in 1078 and 1079. In the last named council he was forced to make a written declaration of his recantation.

165. 'ad hoc verbum substomachus Sanctus': *substomachor* is a Late

Latin word found in Augustine, *Confessiones,* 3.12.21. It means to 'be somewhat peeved, angered,' but anger is still under control.

166. Here follow, ¶¶ 58-62, three accounts where Malachy acts as peacemaker.

167. 'scito me ad tuam paternitatem appellaturum.' The bishop may have been using the term *paternitas* here as an honorary title when addressing his superior. He would, if repulsed, return to Malachy as a son to a loving father. At a somewhat later period *paternitas* was used in a technical legal sense of the right of an abbey over its daughter houses.

168. This is an example of the Old Irish legal institution of 'fasting on a creditor', as a means of securing redress. See Myles Dillon and Nora K. Chadwick, *The Celtic Realms* (New York, 1967) 99.

169. *Scoti sumus, non Galli.* To translate as Lawlor did: 'We are Scots, not Galls', is anachronistic. It would have been proper for Saint Patrick or Saint Columbanus in the fifth or sixth century to have used such language, but not for Saint Bernard in the twelfth. The reference may have been a sarcastic one, referring to the beautiful cathedrals then being built in France. Was this possibly Bernard's criticism of his own people? In this regard see also his comments on richly decorated monasteries: 'I shall say nothing about the soaring heights and extravagant lengths and unnecessary widths of the churches, nothing about their expensive decorations and their novel images, which catch the attention of those who go in to pray, and dry up their devotion.' (*Apo* II,28; SBOp 3:104; CF 1:63).

170. 'et convicium intulit, *simiam* appellans.' He meant that Malachy was an unintelligent imitator (imitating the French in constructing an imposing oratory). The metaphorical use of *simia* is frequent in the twelfth and thirteenth century literature. See E. R. Curtius, *European Literature and the Latin Middle Ages* (London, 1953) Excursus XIX: 'The Ape as Metaphor', 538-540. The Düsseldorf MS here reads *insanum eum,* but it was later erased and corrected.

171. Mk 3:8. It will be noted that here and in ¶ 65 below we have two accounts of Malachy's gift of reading men's thoughts.

172. Apparently it was still the custom that a man entering religion needed the permission of his liege-lord before doing so.

173. *conversus:* anyone making a complete *conversion* in his life-style, embracing the evangelical counsels under vows. The Cistercians were the first to admit *lay brothers,* men under monastic vows to do manual labor, but not bound by choir obligations.

174. This monastery of Inislounaght, close to the River Suir a mile or so west of Clonmel in County Tipperary was known as *De Surio.*

175. Gn 39:17. See the Compline Hymn:

> Procul recedant somnia,
> et noctium phantasmata:
> hostemque nostrum comprime,
> ne polluantur corpora.

176. Some believe that Saint Patrick was buried there, but J. B. Bury, *Life of St. Patrick* (London, 1905) 211, has 'little hesitation that the obscure grave was at Saul'.

177. The implication here seems to be that Patrick was buried there.

178. *'antiquorum* genere *miraculorum . . . .* ' The Gelasian Sacramentary in the Secret for the Mass for Kings has: *'antiqua* brachii tui operare *miracula' (Gelasian Sacramentary* ed. H. A. Wilson [Oxford, 1894] *Missa pro regibus,* 277). See also *Missale Romanum* (Rome, 1956): Missa pro Imperatore [95], where the same secret prayer is printed.

179. He is referring to Ireland. Even in those far-off days the phrase 'bás i nÉrenn' (death in Ireland) was the prayer on many an Irishman's lips when he was in exile or on pilgrimage.

180. He referred of course to Armagh, legendary burial place of Saint Patrick.

181. . . . . diem respondit solemnem omnium defunctorum.

182. See n. 98.

183. Are we to understand from this that the *pallium* represented a sacrament in Malachy's thinking or in that of Bernard? It did indicate a higher order in the hierarchy, certainly not a higher degree of ordination.

184. Pope Eugene III, a former Cistercian monk at Clairvaux, spent the spring of 1148 at Lyons and at Troyes in France.

185. The Pope was in France and there would not be the difficulty of crossing the Alps to Italy. It was the general direction of Clairvaux and Malachy may have had a presentiment of his imminent death.

186. This would have been from Bangor, a day's journey from Scotland (see ¶ 68).

187. 'te in Hiberniam incolumem reversurum.' This is possibly a reminiscence of Horace, *Odes* 1.3:7 where the author prays to the Cyprian goddess to bring back Vergil *safe and sound (reddas incolumem precor).* This was a literary type in classical antiquity, the *propempticon* or 'sending-off poem'. In the Greek and Roman schools students were set to compose such themes as a literary exercise. Some of this training still existed in the twelfth century and formed part of Bernard's early schooling.

188. This was counting from the time when he first left Ireland but was forced back by the storm.

189. The Green Lake. This is the present Soulseat about eight miles from Cairngarroch.

190. The abbot of the Scottish foundation was Michael, mentioned above in ¶15. Bernard told us there that this was Malachy's last monastic foundation.

191. David I of Scotland (1084-1153), a man of great holiness, who founded several Scottish dioceses and introduced the Cistercian Order

to Scotland. Naturally he had much in common with Malachy. See Jhone Leslie, *The Historie of Scotland wrytten first in Latin . . . and translated in Scottish by Father James Dalrymple,* The Scottish Text Society (Edinburgh, 1888) 6:326-28.

192. This was Guisborough in the West Riding of Yorkshire on the Ribble River near the Lancashire border.

193. There was a priory of Augustinian Canons at Guisborough founded by Robert de Brus in 1119.

194. 'canonicam ducentes vitam . . . .' They were canons of St Augustine, hence *vita canonicam* as opposed to *vita monastica* or *eremitica.*

195. It was known that Malachy had spent some time with King David and King Stephen of England was suspicious that Malachy was an emissary of the supporters of the Empress Matilda, his rival to the throne. King David invaded England the following year.

196. King Stephen attempted to prevent Theobald of Canterbury and other bishops from attending the Council of Rheims held in March 1148. However, it is not likely that Malachy had been summoned for that council as he was still in Kent at the time it was held.

197. Pope Eugene had left Clairvaux late in April 1148 (Jaffé, *Regesta,* p. 634).

198. Malachy's prayer had been to die at Clairvaux on November 2. See ¶67.

199. In the *Benedictus* (Lk 1:78) Christ is styled the Orient, the Sunrise. Mediaeval maps showed the British Isles as west of France and Spain, hence Bernard says that Malachy came from the west.

200. Bernard here refers to his weakened condition and his squeamish stomach, something mentioned also by his biographer, William of Saint Thierry, in *Vita Prima* 5:4.

201. Bernard's first eulogy for Saint Malachy mentions that he was to have left for Rome on the feast of Saint Luke (18 October) and that he came down with the fever that same day (*Sermo I de Malachia,* c.1). Some of the manuscripts of the *Vita S. Malachiae* insert: 'On the feast day of blessed Luke the Evangelist when he had celebrated Mass in the convent with that holy devotion which was his . . . .'

202. According to Bernard's first eulogy on Saint Malachy, the physicians themselves saw no sign of immediate death or even of serious illness. (I c. 2.)

203. To die on All Souls' Day would mean that one benefitted from all the prayers of Christendom offered that day for the dead.

204. See the *Usus Antiquiores Ordinis Cisterciensis* 3:94 (PL 166: 1471) for the Cistercian method of administering Extreme Unction.

205. Apparently this was a loft or a balcony opening to the church, on the same level as the dormitory, for the use of the sick and infirm brethren.

206. In a letter written to the monks in Ireland the same month as the death of Malachy, Bernard mentions that Malachy had especially com-

mended the Irish brethren to Bernard's care (Ep. 374 [James, 386]).
207. 'non vultus pallidor, non macilentior videbatur.' *Macilentus* is a post classical word to be found first in Dn 1:10: 'si viderit vultus vestros macilentiores', which may be the source of this passage in Saint Bernard.
208. This does not refer so much to the Feast of All Saints, but to the eternal festival which the saints in Heaven have.
209. 'prosequimur amicum repatriantem.' Bernard in *De considera-tione* 5:2 defines the word *repatrio:* 'This will be a returning home: to have left the land of the body for the region of the spirit which is our God, the supreme spirit, the most sublime dwelling of blessed spirits.' SBOp 3:468, CF 37:141.
210. AFM 2:1085 a.1148 says that he was in the fifty-fourth year of his age. It further mentions that he was buried at Clairvaux with great honor and solemnity.
211. The *Vita Prima* 4:21 tells us that Bernard was the celebrant and he used the collect for the commemoration of bishops instead of the prayer for the dead, knowing full well that Saint Malachy's canoniza-tion would follow in a short time.
121. Mt 17:5. Some of the manuscripts identify this as 'the oratory of Mary the Mother of God', the special patroness of the Cistercian Order.
213. 2 Tm 1:12. *Depositum* = mortal remains and a deposit made for safekeeping.
214. Bernard uses the term *contubernalio,* an old Latin military term meaning: 'one who shares the same tent, a comrade in arms'. The monk was, after all, a soldier enlisted in a great army fighting the devil and the world.

SERMON ON THE PASSING OF MALACHY

215. Lm 4:4. This is an inexact quotation. The Vulgate says: '. . . and there was none to break it unto them.'
216. Bernard means that it seemed divine intervention that the delays in the journey prevented Malachy from reaching Rome, the goal of his pilgrimage, but he died and was buried at Clairvaux as he had wished.
217. Apparently the new monastery at Clairvaux had been completed and the remains of Cistercians were moved into the new cemetery at this time. The rebuilding of Clairvaux began about 1135 and was com-pleted by 1149. See Archdale King, *Citeaux and her elder daughters* (London, 1954) 236 f.
218. *Vita Bern* 4:21 informs us that at the end of the funeral Mass St Bernard had devoutly kissed Malachy's feet.
219. This is a very old metaphor. St Bernard has often been called

'the last of the Fathers', as he not only knew Scripture well but was well acquainted with patristic writers. Rufinus, *Commentaries in Symbolum Apostolorum,* c.16 may have been Bernard's ultimate source: 'When a fish, for example, seizes a hook concealed in bait, it not only cannot remove the bait from the hook, but is itself dragged out of the deep to become bait for other fish. In precisely the same way, when he who had the power of death seized the body of Jesus, he failed to notice the hook of Deity enclosed within it: so, when he swallowed it, he was immediately caught and, bursting the bars of the underworld, was dragged out from the abyss to become a bait for others.' tr. J. N. D. Kelly, *Rufinus, A Commentary on the Apostle's Creed,* ACW 20 (London, 1955) 51, 120. Rufinus may have derived this from Gregory of Nyssa, *Oratio Catechetica,* 24. See the edition of J.H. Scrawley (Cambridge, 1903: CPT) 93, who quotes Gregory the Great, *Moralia* 33:7, in commenting on Job 40:19: ' . . . in hamo ergo ejus incarnationis captus est, quia dum in illo appetit escam corporis, transfixus est aculeo divinitatis.' Bernard had used this before in SC 26:11: 'You are dead, O death, pierced by the hook you have incautiously swallowed, even as the Prophet said: "O death, I will be your death; O hell, I will be your destruction." Pierced by that hook, you open a broad and happy exit to life for the faithful who pass through your midst.' (Tr. Kilian Walsh, CF 7:70-71).

220. Ho 13:14. This occurs also in the antiphon for the First Vespers of the Feast of the Exaltation of the Holy Cross (14 September): O magnum pietatis opus: mors mortua tunc est, in ligno quando mortua vita fuit.

221. Ws 3:3. This occurs also in the Communion of the Mass for the Vigil of All Saints (October 31): visi sunt oculis insipientium mori; illi autem sunt in pace (*Missale Romanum,* 734). St. Bernard changed it to 'nimirum visus est oculis insipientium mori, ille autem est in pace'.

222. *examinavit non exinanivit,* a pun (paronomasia), a favorite rhetorical device of St Bernard. The very beginning of *Life* has a pun, a play on words: See *Life* ¶1, fn. 5.

HOMILY ON THE DEATH OF SAINT MALACHY

223. It is clear from ¶7 that Bernard preached this homily on the anniversary of Malachy's death. He wrote the *Life* that year and there are passages here and in the *Life* that coincide very closely with this homily which was originally called 'The second sermon on the Passing of Malachy'.

224. The words *peregrinus* and *exsilium* both echo the Church Fathers; we are on pilgrimage as strangers here on earth; our true home is

heaven for which we should strive.

225. See *Life* ¶33: 'the loving father of all . . . . ' So also of Malchus who taught Malachy, *Life* ¶8: 'he was reverenced by all, as the one father of all.'

226. St Bernard's rhetorical device: *patiens . . . compatiens . . . impatiens . . .* hardly admits of exact English translation.

227. St Bernard's pun (*non urebatur illa sed utebatur*) cannot be reproduced in English.

228. . . . . *diceris patriae natum non sibi.* This is a possible reminiscence of Lucan, *Pharsalia* 2:382-3 (of the older Cato):

> naturamque sequi *patriae*que inpendere vitam
> nec *sibi* sed toti genitum se credere mundo

('to follow nature, to give his life for his country, to believe that he was born to serve the whole world and not himself.') trans. J. D. Duff, Lucan: *The Civil War,* Loeb Classical Library (London, 1928) 84-85.

229. *Sine turbatione versabatur in turbis . . .*

230. The word *otium* is used here in its monastic sense: Bernard elsewhere employs the term *negotiosissimum otium*—'a very busy leisure', as Dom Jean Leclercq translates it. (*The Love of Learning and the Desire for God,* trans. C. Misrahi [New York, 1961] 35, 73.) Since it anticipates eternal rest, the monastic life is a life of leisure, withdrawn from the world, but a life of activity as well, a life whose every moment is regulated. Cf. Csi 4:12 'in ease not taking ease', and *Life* ¶43.

231. At this point several of the manuscripts have a passage interpolated from the first sermon *De transitu . . .* ¶5, some nine lines in the critical edition.

232. *sanctus Pontifex:* at this time *pontifex* meant simply 'bishop'. See the article by S. E. Donlon, 'Pontiff' in NCE 11:549.

INDEX

INDEX

CISTERCIAN PUBLICATIONS, INC.
TITLES LISTING

—CISTERCIAN TEXTS—

BERNARD OF CLAIRVAUX

Apologia to Abbot William
Bernard of Clairvaux, Letters of
Five Books on Consideration: Advice to a
    Pope
Homilies in Praise of the Blessed Virgin Mary
Life and Death of Saint Malachy the Irishman
Love without Measure: Extracts from the
    Writings of St Bernard (Paul Dimier)
On Grace and Free Choice
On Loving God (Analysis by Emero
    Stiegman)
Parables and Sentences (Michael Casey)
Sermons for the Summer Season
Sermons on Conversion
Sermons on the Song of Songs I–IV
The Steps of Humility and Pride

WILLIAM OF SAINT THIERRY

The Enigma of Faith
Exposition on the Epistle to the Romans
Exposition on the Song of Songs
The Golden Epistle
The Mirror of Faith
The Nature and Dignity of Love
On Contemplating God: Prayer &
    Meditations

AELRED OF RIEVAULX

Dialogue on the Soul
Liturgical Sermons, I
Mirror of Charity
Spiritual Friendship
Treatises I: On Jesus at the Age of Twelve,
    Rule for a Recluse, The Pastoral Prayer
Walter Daniel: The Life of Aelred of Rievaulx

JOHN OF FORD

Sermons on the Final Verses of the
    Songs of Songs I–VII

GILBERT OF HOYLAND

Sermons on the Songs of Songs I–III
Treatises, Sermons and Epistles

OTHER EARLY
CISTERCIAN WRITERS

Adam of Perseigne, Letters of
Alan of Lille: The Art of Preaching
Amadeus of Lausanne: Homilies in Praise of
    Blessed Mary
Baldwin of Ford: Spiritual Tractates I–II
Gertrud the Greata: Spiritual Exercises

Gertrud the Great: The Herald of God's
    Loving-Kindness
Guerric of Igny: Liturgical Sermons I–[II]
Helinand of Froidmont: Verses on Death
Idung of Prüfening: Cistercians and Cluniacs:
    The Case of Cîteaux
Isaac of Stella: Sermons on the Christian
    Year,
    I–[II]
The Life of Beatrice of Nazareth
Serlo of Wilton & Serlo of Savigny: Seven
    Unpublished Works
Stephen of Lexington: Letters from Ireland
Stephen of Sawley: Treatises

—MONASTIC TEXTS—

EASTERN CHRISTIAN TRADITION

Besa: The Life of Shenoute
Cyril of Scythopolis: Lives of the Monks of
    Palestine
Dorotheos of Gaza: Discourses and Sayings
Evagrius Ponticus: Praktikos and Chapters on
    Prayer
Handmaids of the Lord: Lives of Holy
    Women in Late Antiquity & Early
    Middle Ages (Joan Petersen)
Harlots of the Desert (Benedicta Ward)
John Moschos: The Spiritual Meadow
Lives of the Desert Fathers
Lives of Simeon Stylites (Robert Doran)
Luminous Eye (Sebastian Brock)
Mena of Nikiou: Isaac of Alexandra & St
    Macrobius
Pachomian Koinonia I–III (Armand Veilleux)
Paphnutius: Histories/Monks of Upper
    Egypt
Sayings of the Desert Fathers
    (Benedicta Ward)
Spiritual Direction in the Early Christian
    East
    (Irénée Hausherr)
Spiritually Beneficial Tales of Paul, Bishop of
    Monembasia (John Wortley)
Symeon the New Theologian: The
    Theological and Practical Treatises &
    The Three Theological Discourses (Paul
    McGuckin)
Theodoret of Cyrrhus: A History of the
    Monks of Syria
The Syriac Fathers on Prayer and the
    Spiritual Life (Sebastian Brock)

WESTERN   CHRISTIAN
TRADITION

Anselm of Canterbury: Letters I–III
    (Walter Fröhlich)

CISTERCIAN PUBLICATIONS, INC.
TITLES LISTING

Bede: Commentary...Acts of the Apostles
Bede: Commentary...Seven Catholic Epistles
Bede: Homilies on the Gospels III
The Celtic Monk (U. O Maidín)
Gregory the Great: Forty Gospel Homilies
Life of the Jura Fathers
Maxims of Stephen of Muret
Meditations of Guigo I, Prior of the
   Charterhouse (A. Gordon Mursell)
Peter of Celle: Selected Works
Letters of Rancé I–II
Rule of the Master
Rule of Saint Augustine
Wound of Love: A Carthusian Miscellany

CHRISTIAN SPIRITUALITY

Cloud of Witnesses: The Development of
   Christian Doctrine (David N. Bell)
Call of Wild Geese (Matthew Kelty)
Cistercian Way (André Louf)
The Contemplative Path
Drinking From the Hidden Fountain
   (Thomas Špidlík)
Eros and Allegory: Medieval Exegesis of the
   Song of Songs (Denys Turner)
Fathers Talking (Aelred Squire)
Friendship and Community (Brian McGuire)
From Cloister to Classroom
Life of St Mary Magdalene and of Her Sister
   St Martha (David Mycoff)
Many Mansions (David N. Bell)
Mercy in Weakness (André Louf)
Name of Jesus (Irénée Hausherr)
No Moment Too Small (Norvene Vest)
Penthos: The Doctrine of Compunction in
   the Christian East (Irénée Hausherr)
Rancé and the Trappist Legacy
   (A.J. Krailsheimer)
Russian Mystics (Sergius Bolshakoff)
Sermons in a Monastery (Matthew Kelty)
Silent Herald of Unity: The Life of
   Maria Gabrielle Sagheddu (Martha
   Driscoll)
Spirituality of the Christian East
   (Thomas Špidlík)
Spirituality of the Medieval West
   (André Vauchez)
Tuning In To Grace (André Louf)
Wholly Animals: A Book of Beastly Tales
   (David N. Bell)

—MONASTIC STUDIES—

Community and Abbot in the Rule of
   St Benedict I–II (Adalbert De Vogüé)
Finances of the Cistercian Order in the
   Fourteenth Century (Peter King)
Fountains Abbey and Its Benefactors
   (Joan Wardrop)

The Hermit Monks of Grandmont
   (Carole A. Hutchison)
In the Unity of the Holy Spirit
   (Sighard Kleiner)
Joy of Learning & the Love of God:
   Essays in Honor of Jean Leclercq
Monastic Odyssey (Marie Kervingant)
Monastic Practices (Charles Cummings)
Occupation of Celtic Sites in Ireland
   (Geraldine Carville)
Reading St Benedict (Adalbert de Vogüé)
Rule of St Benedict: A Doctrinal and Spiritual
   Commentary (Adalbert de Vogüé)
Rule of St Benedict (Br. Pinocchio)
St Hugh of Lincoln (David H. Farmer)
Stones Laid Before the Lord (Anselme
   Dimier)
Venerable Bede (Benedicta Ward)
What Nuns Read (David N. Bell)
With Greater Liberty: A Short History of
   Christian Monasticism & Religious
   Orders (Karl Frank)

—CISTERCIAN STUDIES—

Aelred of Rievaulx: A Study (Aelred Squire)
Athirst for God: Spiritual Desire in Bernard
   of Clairvaux's Sermons on the Song of
   Songs (Michael Casey)
Beatrice of Nazareth in Her Context
   (Roger De Ganck)
Bernard of Clairvaux: Man, Monk, Mystic
   (Michael Casey) [tapes and readings]
Bernardus Magister (Nonacentenary)
Catalogue of Manuscripts in the Obrecht
   Collection of the Institute of Cistercian
   Studies (Anna Kirkwood)
Christ the Way: The Christology of Guerric
   of Igny (John Morson)
Cistercians in Denmark (Brian McGuire)
Cistercians in Medieval Art (James France)
Cistercians in Scandinavia (James France)
A Difficult Saint (Brian McGuire)
Dore Abbey (Shoesmith & Richardson)
A Gathering of Friends: Learning &
   Spirituality in John of Forde (Costello
   and Holdsworth)
Image and Likeness: The Augustinian
   Spirituality of William of St Thierry
   (David Bell)
Index of Authors & Works in Cistercian
   Libraries in Great Britain I (David Bell)
Index of Cistercian Authors and Works in
   Medieval Library Catalogues in Great
   Britian (David Bell)
Mystical Theology of St Bernard
   (Étienne Gilson)
The New Monastery: Texts & Studies on the
   Earliest Cistercians

CISTERCIAN PUBLICATIONS, INC.
TITLES LISTING

Nicolas Cotheret's Annals of Cîteaux
(Louis J. Lekai)
Pater Bernhardus (Franz Posset)
A Second Look at Saint Bernard
(Jean Leclercq)
The Spiritual Teachings of St Bernard of
Clairvaux (John R. Sommerfeldt)
Studies in Medieval Cistercian History
(various)
Studiosorum Speculum (Louis J. Lekai)
Three Founders of Cîteaux
(Jean-Baptiste Van Damme)
Towards Unification with God (Beatrice of
Nazareth in Her Context, 2)
William, Abbot of St Thierry
Women and St Bernard of Clairvaux
(Jean Leclercq)

MEDIEVAL RELIGIOUS —WOMEN—

Lillian Thomas Shank and John A. Nichols, editors
Distant Echoes
Hidden Springs: Cistercian Monastic Women
(2 volumes)
Peace Weavers

—CARTHUSIAN— TRADITION

Call of Silent Love (A Carthusian)
Freedom of Obedience (A Carthusian)
Guigo II: The Ladder of Monks & Twelve
Meditations (Colledge & Walsh)
Interior Prayer (A Carthusian)
Meditations of Guigo II (A. Gorden Mursell)
Prayer of Love and Silence (A Carthusian)
Way of Silent Love (A Carthusian Miscellany)
Wound of Love (A Carthusian Miscellany)
They Speak by Silences (A Carthusian)
Where Silence is Praise (A Carthusian)

—STUDIES IN CISTERCIAN— ART & ARCHITECTURE

Meredith Parsons Lillich, editor
Volumes II–V are now available

—THOMAS MERTON—

The Climate of Monastic Prayer (T. Merton)
The Legacy of Thomas Merton (P. Hart)
The Message of Thomas Merton (P. Hart)
The Monastic Journey of Thomas Merton
(P. Hart)
Thomas Merton/Monk (P. Hart)
Thomas Merton on St Bernard
Toward an Integrated Humanity
(M. Basil Pennington, ed.)

CISTERCIAN LITURGICAL —DOCUMENTS SERIES—

Chrysogonus Waddell, ocso, editor
Hymn Collection of the...Paraclete
Institutiones nostrae: The Paraclete Statutes
Molesme Summer-Season Breviary (4 vols.)
Old French Ordinary & Breviary of the
Abbey of the Paraclete (2 volumes)
Twelfth-century Cistercian Hymnal (2 vols.)
The Twelfth-century Cistercian Psalter
Two Early Cistercian *Libelli Missarum*

–STUDIA PATRISTICA XVIII–

Volumes 1, 2 and 3

❖❖❖❖❖❖❖❖❖❖❖❖❖

*Editorial queries & advance book information
should be directed to the Editorial Offices:*

Cistercian Publications
1201 Oliver Street
Western Michigan University
Kalamazoo, Michigan 49008
Tel: (616) 387-8920 • Fax: (616) 387-8921

*Cistercian Publications is a non-profit
corporation. Its publishing program is restricted
to monastic texts in translation and books on
the monastic tradition.*

•••

*North American customers may order these
books through booksellers or directly by
contacting the warehouse at the address below:*

Cistercian Publications
Saint Joseph's Abbey
167 North Spencer Road
Spencer, Massachusetts 01562-1233
Tel: (508) 885-8730 • Fax: (508) 885-4687
email: cistpub@spencerabbey.org

•••

British & European Orders:

Cistercian Publications
Mount Saint Bernard Abbey
Coalville, Leicester LE67 5UL
Fax: [44] (1530) 81.46.08

•••

*A complete catalogue of texts in translation and
studies on early, medieval, and modern
monasticism is available, free of charge, by
contacting any of the addresses above.*